World War II Stories for Kids

15 Action-Packed and Inspiring Stories from Some of the Most Remarkable Figures of WWII

Clara Truheart

AF406391

Copyright

All rights reserved. No part of this book may be reproduced, stored in a retrieval system, or transmitted in any form or by any means, electronic, mechanical, photocopying, recording, or otherwise, without the prior written permission of the publisher, except for brief quotations used in reviews.

This book is a work of nonfiction. Any similarity to real persons, living or dead, is coincidental and not intended by the author.

© 2024 by Clara Truheart

Disclaimer

The stories contained in "World War II Stories for Kids: 15 Action-Packed and Inspiring Stories from Some of the Most Remarkable Figures of WWII" are based on historical events and real figures from World War II. While every effort has been made to ensure the accuracy of the events described, certain elements have been simplified or adapted to make them more accessible and understandable for young readers. Some characters and dialogues may have been fictionalized for narrative purposes. The content is intended for educational and entertainment use only and should not be considered a definitive historical account. Parents

and guardians are encouraged to discuss the topics
covered in this book with children to provide
additional context and understanding.

Table of Contents

What This Book is About

"History is not a burden on the memory but an illumination of the soul." These words, spoken by Lord Acton, perfectly encapsulate the spirit of this book. Within these pages, you will find stories that are not just about war, but about the incredible courage, resilience, and humanity that shone through even in the darkest times of World War II. This book is designed to transport young readers into the past, offering them a glimpse into the lives of those who stood tall in the face of overwhelming odds.

World War II was a global conflict that involved over 30 countries and lasted from 1939 to 1945. It was a time of immense turmoil, fear, and destruction, but it was also a period where ordinary people performed extraordinary acts of bravery. These stories are a testament to the indomitable human spirit, to the belief that even in the midst of war, there is room for goodness, friendship, and hope. The heroes of these tales are not just soldiers; they are children, women, animals, and ordinary men who, through their actions, left a mark on history.

Imagine being a child during World War II. Schools were often disrupted, cities were bombed, and families were torn apart. Yet, even in such circumstances, young people found ways to contribute to the war effort, to help others, and to stand up for what was right. One of the stories you'll read about is that of Anne Frank, a young girl whose diary has become one of the most poignant accounts of life during the war. Anne's story is not just a tale of survival but one of unyielding hope, showing that even in the face of unimaginable fear, a person can still dream of a better world.

Another story that will captivate you is that of the Navajo Code Talkers, a group of Native

American soldiers who used their unique language to create an unbreakable code that played a crucial role in the Allied victory. Their story is one of ingenuity and courage, showing how cultural heritage became a vital weapon in a global war. Similarly, the story of Irena Sendler, a Polish woman who saved 2,500 Jewish children from the Holocaust, highlights the power of compassion and the risks some were willing to take to protect the innocent.

In addition to these stories of human bravery, the book also delves into the remarkable contributions of animals during the war. From Smoky, the tiny dog who became a hero by saving lives through her fearless work, to

Wojtek, a bear who fought alongside Polish soldiers, these tales remind us that courage comes in all shapes and sizes.

Why WWII Still Matters Today

"Those who cannot remember the past are condemned to repeat it." This famous quote by philosopher George Santayana serves as a powerful reminder of the importance of understanding history, especially when it comes to events as significant as World War II. For many, the war might seem like a distant chapter in the history books, a series of battles and events that happened long before they were born. However, the impact of WWII continues to shape the world we live in today, influencing everything from international relations to our understanding of justice, courage, and the resilience of the human spirit.

World War II was not just a conflict between nations; it was a global struggle that tested the limits of human endurance and morality. The war brought out the best and the worst in humanity, showcasing acts of unimaginable cruelty alongside stories of profound kindness and bravery. These stories, many of which are highlighted in this book, offer valuable lessons that remain relevant today. They remind us of the cost of hatred and intolerance, the power of unity and cooperation, and the importance of standing up for what is right, even in the face of overwhelming odds.

The consequences of World War II are still visible in the geopolitical landscape of the 21st century. The war led to the establishment of the United Nations, an international organization created to prevent future conflicts and promote peace and cooperation among nations. The ideals of the UN, such as the protection of human rights and the promotion of social progress, were born out of the horrors of WWII. The war also reshaped national borders, created new alliances, and set the stage for the Cold War, a period of tension between the United States and the Soviet Union that lasted for decades. Understanding these outcomes helps us make sense of current global issues and conflicts.

But beyond the political and social ramifications, World War II teaches us about the strength of the human spirit. The stories of those who lived through the war—soldiers, civilians, and children alike—are stories of survival, determination, and hope. These individuals faced unimaginable hardships, yet they found ways to persevere, to protect others, and to hold onto their humanity in the darkest of times. Their stories inspire us to be brave in the face of adversity, to help others whenever we can, and to believe in the possibility of a better future, no matter how bleak the present may seem.

The lessons of World War II are not just about the past; they are about the future. They teach us the importance of remembering history, of honoring those who fought and suffered, and of ensuring that the mistakes of the past are not repeated. As we share these stories with the next generation, we pass on the values of courage, kindness, and resilience. We remind young readers that they, too, have the power to make a difference in the world, just as the remarkable figures of WWII did. And in doing so, we help build a world where peace, understanding, and justice can prevail, even in the most challenging of times.

The purpose of this book is to inspire young readers, to show them that even in the most difficult times, there is always the possibility to make a difference. The stories are action-packed, filled with moments of tension, bravery, and triumph. They are stories of people who refused to give up, who believed in something greater than themselves, and who, through their actions, changed the course of history. This is not just a book about World War II; it is a collection of life lessons, a reminder that in the midst of chaos, there is always hope, always a chance to be a hero in your own right. These stories are as relevant today as they were during the war, and they serve as a powerful reminder of the strength and resilience that lies within each of us.

How to Use This Book

World War II was one of the most significant events of the 20th century, shaping the world in ways that are still felt today. It was a time when ordinary people were thrust into extraordinary circumstances, where the line between good and evil was drawn with stark clarity. But beyond the headlines of battles and political maneuvers, there were countless individuals whose acts of bravery and kindness made a difference, often in the most unexpected ways. This book is a celebration of those individuals, bringing to life the incredible tales of heroism and resilience that emerged during those tumultuous years.

Imagine being a young pilot in the Battle of Britain, barely out of your teens, tasked with defending your country from an enemy that seemed unstoppable. Or picture the bravery of a young girl like Anne Frank, who, despite being confined in a small attic, maintained hope and courage that continue to inspire millions today. These are not just stories of war; they are stories of people—young and old, male and female, from all corners of the globe—who stood up against fear and oppression. Their stories are a testament to the indomitable spirit of humanity, proving that even in the darkest times, there is always light.

For children, understanding the complexities of World War II can be challenging. The facts and figures, while important, do not capture the emotional depth of the experiences lived by those who were there. This book seeks to bridge that gap, presenting stories that are not only informative but also deeply moving. Each tale has been carefully selected to resonate with young readers, to help them see beyond the history lessons and into the hearts of the people who lived through the war.

These are not just tales of soldiers and battles. They are also stories of ordinary civilians who performed extraordinary acts of courage. There's the story of Irena Sendler, who risked her life to save thousands of Jewish children from the horrors of the Holocaust. Or the tale of the Navajo Code Talkers, whose unique language became an unbreakable code that helped secure victory in the Pacific. Each story is a reminder that heroism comes in many forms, and that even the smallest acts of kindness can have a profound impact.

As young readers dive into these pages, they will meet the heroes who defied the odds, who showed that bravery is not just about facing danger on the battlefield, but also about standing up for what is right, even when it is difficult. They will learn that World War II was not just a time of destruction, but also a time of incredible resilience and humanity. Through these stories, children will gain a deeper understanding of the values that mattered then—and that still matter today: courage, friendship, and the unwavering belief in the goodness of people.

This book invites young readers to embark on a journey through history, one that is filled with adventure, emotion, and inspiration. Each story is a window into the past, offering a glimpse of the lives that were touched by World War II and the remarkable people who left their mark on history. The lessons learned from these stories are timeless, teaching us that no matter the circumstances, the human spirit has the power to overcome adversity and make a difference in the world.

Chapter One

The Spark of War

The Road to WWII: Understanding the Conflict

World War II was one of the most significant events in human history, shaping the world in ways that are still felt today. But to understand the incredible stories of bravery, friendship, and courage that emerged from this conflict, it's important to first grasp how the war began. The road to World War II was paved with a series of events, decisions, and actions that gradually led the world into a state of conflict. This journey wasn't sudden; it was the result of tensions that had been building for years, fueled by the aftermath of World War I, economic instability, and the rise of powerful leaders who would change the course of history.

At the end of World War I in 1918, the world hoped for lasting peace. The Treaty of Versailles was signed in 1919 to officially end the war, and it placed heavy penalties on Germany, blaming it for the war and demanding reparations. Germany lost territories, had its military severely restricted, and was forced to pay enormous sums of money to the Allied powers. This treaty, meant to secure peace, instead sowed the seeds of resentment and anger. Many Germans felt humiliated and betrayed, believing that the treaty was unfair and too harsh. This widespread discontent created fertile ground for radical ideas and leaders to take root.

As Germany struggled under the weight of the treaty and the global economic depression that followed in the 1930s, Adolf Hitler rose to power. Hitler was a charismatic leader who promised to restore Germany to its former glory. He spoke passionately about reversing the Treaty of Versailles, rebuilding the military, and expanding German territory. His ideas were extreme and dangerous, but they resonated with a population desperate for change. In 1933, Hitler became Chancellor of Germany, and soon after, he consolidated his power, transforming Germany into a dictatorship. He and his Nazi Party quickly set about rearming Germany, violating the Treaty of Versailles.

While Hitler was gaining power in Germany, other parts of the world were also experiencing significant changes. In Italy, Benito Mussolini, a dictator who believed in the superiority of the Italian nation, had taken control. Like Hitler, Mussolini was intent on expanding his country's influence and territory. Meanwhile, in Japan, a militaristic government was pushing for expansion throughout Asia. These three countries—Germany, Italy, and Japan—formed an alliance known as the Axis Powers, united by their desire to expand their empires and their opposition to the Allied nations, which included Britain, France, and later the United States and the Soviet Union.

The world watched with growing concern as Hitler's ambitions became clearer. In 1936, German troops marched into the Rhineland, a region that had been demilitarized under the Treaty of Versailles. This bold move was a direct violation of the treaty, but the response from other European nations was muted. Many leaders were still haunted by the horrors of World War I and were desperate to avoid another conflict. They believed that by appeasing Hitler, by allowing him to take small steps unchecked, they could prevent a full-scale war. This policy of appeasement, however, only emboldened Hitler.

Emboldened by the lack of resistance, Hitler continued to push his agenda. In 1938, he annexed Austria, claiming that he was uniting all German-speaking people under one nation. The world again did nothing, hoping that this would be the end of his territorial ambitions. But Hitler had much larger plans. Later that year, he demanded control of the Sudetenland, a region of Czechoslovakia with a large German-speaking population. The Munich Agreement, signed by Britain, France, Germany, and Italy, allowed Hitler to take the Sudetenland in exchange for a promise of no further territorial expansion. This agreement, like previous attempts to appease Hitler, only served to delay the inevitable.

In March 1939, just months after the Munich Agreement, Hitler broke his promise and invaded the rest of Czechoslovakia. The world was now beginning to see that appeasement had failed. Hitler's ambitions were not limited to uniting German-speaking people; he sought to conquer Europe. Britain and France, realizing the futility of further negotiations, began preparing for the possibility of war. They promised to defend Poland, Hitler's next likely target, should Germany attack.

The final straw came on September 1, 1939, when Germany invaded Poland. This invasion was swift and brutal, employing a new military tactic known as Blitzkrieg, or "lightning war," which involved rapid, overwhelming force to quickly defeat the enemy. Britain and France, honoring their commitment to Poland, declared war on Germany two days later. World War II had officially begun.

As the war progressed, it became clear that this was not just a European conflict but a global one. Japan, already engaged in aggressive expansion in Asia, attacked the United States at Pearl Harbor in December 1941, drawing America into the war. The Soviet Union, initially neutral, was invaded by Germany in 1941, bringing it into the conflict on the side of the Allies. The war would go on to engulf nations across the world, resulting in unprecedented destruction and loss of life.

The road to World War II was marked by a series of calculated moves by aggressive leaders, the reluctance of other nations to confront these threats early on, and the deep-seated anger left over from World War I. Understanding this path is crucial to appreciating the remarkable stories of heroism, sacrifice, and resilience that emerged during the war. These stories, set against the backdrop of a world in turmoil, remind us of the importance of standing up to tyranny, the power of unity, and the enduring human spirit in the face of unimaginable challenges. As we explore these tales, we gain insight not only into the past but also into the values that continue to shape our world today.

The Invasion of Poland: The War Begins

In the early hours of September 1, 1939, a quiet morning in Poland was shattered by the roar of airplanes and the rumble of tanks. This was the day that marked the beginning of World War II, a conflict that would change the world forever. The peaceful towns and villages of Poland suddenly found themselves under attack by a powerful and well-prepared enemy. This invasion, known as the invasion of Poland, was the spark that ignited a war that would involve nearly every nation on Earth.

Poland, at that time, was a proud and independent country. It had its own government, its own army, and a rich culture that went back hundreds of years. The people of Poland were hard-working, resilient, and deeply patriotic. But they were not prepared for the might of the

German war machine that was about to descend upon them.

Germany, led by a man named Adolf Hitler, had been preparing for this moment for years. Hitler had risen to power by promising to restore Germany's former glory, and he believed that expanding Germany's territory was the way to achieve that. Poland was his first target. With a powerful army and advanced weaponry, Hitler was confident that his forces could crush Poland quickly and efficiently.

As the German forces advanced, the Polish people were caught off guard. The invasion began with a tactic known as "Blitzkrieg," or "lightning war." This was a new and terrifying way of fighting. German airplanes bombed cities, railways, and communication centers, while tanks and troops quickly moved in to take control. The Polish army, though brave and determined, was no match for the speed and power of the German assault. They fought valiantly, but they were outnumbered and outgunned.

In the first days of the invasion, the skies over Poland were filled with German planes, their engines roaring as they dropped bombs on towns and cities. The sound of explosions echoed across the land, and the people of Poland knew that their lives would never be the same. Buildings crumbled, fires raged, and panic spread. Families were torn apart as they tried to flee to safety. The roads were clogged with refugees, all desperately seeking shelter from the relentless onslaught.

Despite the overwhelming odds, the Polish soldiers fought back with everything they had. In the forests, on the plains, and in the cities, they resisted the German forces with courage and determination. Stories of their bravery began to spread. There was the story of the defenders of Westerplatte, a small Polish garrison that held out against the German army for seven days, despite being outnumbered and outgunned. These soldiers became symbols of Polish resistance and defiance.

In the city of Warsaw, the Polish capital, the people refused to give up. They built barricades in the streets and took up arms to defend their homes. The battle for Warsaw was fierce and bloody. The Germans bombarded the city from the air, but the Poles fought back, street by street, building by building. Even as the situation grew more desperate, the people of Warsaw remained determined to resist.

However, the German army was not the only enemy Poland faced. To the east, the Soviet Union, under the leadership of Joseph Stalin, also had its eyes on Poland. Just 17 days after the German invasion began, Soviet forces crossed Poland's eastern border. The Polish army, already stretched thin by the German attack, now found itself fighting a war on two fronts. The situation was dire.

The invasion of Poland was swift and brutal. By the end of September, the country had been divided between Germany and the Soviet Union. The Polish government was forced to flee, and the country was occupied by two of the most powerful and oppressive regimes the world had ever known. But even in defeat, the spirit of the Polish people was not broken.

The invasion of Poland was not just the beginning of World War II; it was also the beginning of a long and difficult struggle for the people of Poland. Under German occupation, the

Polish people faced unimaginable hardships. The Nazis implemented harsh measures to control the population, and many Poles were arrested, imprisoned, or killed. Jewish communities in Poland, which had flourished for centuries, were targeted for extermination. The horrors of the Holocaust began to unfold, and millions of innocent lives were lost.

But amid the darkness, there were also incredible acts of heroism and kindness. Ordinary people risked their lives to save others. The Polish resistance movement, made up of men, women, and even children, carried out daring missions to sabotage the German war effort and protect their fellow citizens. They smuggled food and supplies to those in need, gathered intelligence for the Allies, and organized underground schools and newspapers to keep the spirit of freedom alive.

One of the most remarkable figures to emerge from this time was Irena Sendler, a Polish social worker who saved the lives of over 2,500 Jewish children by smuggling them out of the Warsaw Ghetto. Disguised as a nurse, she transported children in ambulances, buried them in coffins, and even hid them in toolboxes to get them to safety. Her bravery and selflessness became legendary, and she is remembered as one of the greatest heroes of World War II.

The story of the invasion of Poland is a story of courage, resilience, and the unbreakable human spirit. It is a story that shows us that even in the darkest of times, there is always hope. The Polish people, though defeated militarily, never gave up their fight for freedom. Their resistance inspired others across Europe and played a crucial role in the eventual defeat of the Nazis.

As we remember the invasion of Poland and the beginning of World War II, we must also remember the lessons it teaches us. We must remember the importance of standing up against tyranny and oppression, of fighting for what is right, even when the odds are against us. And we must remember the incredible power of ordinary people to make a difference in the world, even in the face of unimaginable challenges.

This chapter in history, though filled with pain and suffering, is also filled with stories of hope, bravery, and the enduring strength of the human spirit. It is these stories that we should carry with us, as reminders of the courage it takes to stand up for what is right, and the impact that even the smallest acts of kindness can have on the world.

Chapter Two

A Soldier's Best Friend

The Tale of Smoky: The Brave Little Dog

In the thick of World War II, where bravery was often measured by the size of one's heart rather than physical strength, a small, four-pound Yorkshire Terrier named Smoky proved that even the tiniest creatures could make a monumental impact. Smoky's journey from an abandoned pup in the dense jungles of New Guinea to a decorated war hero is a tale of courage, loyalty, and the extraordinary bond between a dog and her handler, Corporal William A. Wynne.

The story of Smoky began in 1944, when a U.S. soldier stumbled upon the tiny dog in a foxhole. Abandoned and seemingly forgotten, Smoky was a mere shadow of herself, with matted fur and a frail body that spoke of weeks, perhaps months, of fending for herself in the wild. The soldier, unsure of what to do with the little dog, decided to sell her to Corporal Wynne for two Australian pounds. Little did he know that this simple transaction would mark the beginning of a remarkable friendship and an incredible wartime adventure.

Smoky quickly became more than just a pet to Wynne; she became his constant companion and, eventually, his savior. The two formed an unbreakable bond, with Smoky accompanying Wynne on missions across the Pacific Theater. Wherever Wynne went, Smoky was by his side, riding in his backpack, peeking out with her bright, inquisitive eyes, or running alongside him through the dense jungle. Despite her small size, Smoky had the heart of a lion, and her bravery soon became legendary among the troops.

One of Smoky's most notable contributions to the war effort occurred on the island of Luzon in the Philippines. Allied forces needed to run a communications cable through a narrow, 70-foot-long culvert under an airstrip. The task was daunting; sending a soldier through the pipe would expose them to enemy fire, and it was crucial to avoid delays that could compromise the mission. That's when Wynne came up with a daring idea. He knew Smoky was small enough to fit through the pipe, and if she could be coaxed to carry the cable through, it would save time and lives.

Wynne carefully tied the cable to Smoky's collar and gently urged her into the pipe. The little dog hesitated only for a moment before bravely venturing into the darkness. Wynne and the other soldiers held their breath, anxiously waiting as Smoky disappeared into the narrow tunnel. Moments stretched into what felt like hours, but finally, on the other side of the airstrip, Smoky emerged, dragging the cable behind her. The mission was a success, and Smoky had saved the day. Her courageous act allowed the soldiers to establish critical communications, likely preventing countless casualties and ensuring the success of their operations.

Smoky's heroism didn't end there. She continued to serve alongside Wynne, providing more than just practical assistance. In the often bleak and frightening world of war, Smoky was a source of joy and comfort to the soldiers. She became a mascot of sorts, boosting morale wherever she went. Her small stature and playful demeanor brought smiles to the faces of battle-weary troops, reminding them of the innocence and goodness that still existed despite the horrors of war. Smoky would perform tricks, like walking on a tightrope made from a string or riding in a soldier's helmet as if it were a makeshift car, all to the delight of the men who had grown to love her.

Smoky's contributions to the war effort were recognized by the military, and she was awarded eight battle stars, a testament to her involvement in key operations across the Pacific. But beyond the medals and accolades, Smoky's true legacy lay in the hearts of the men she served alongside. To them, she was more than a dog; she was a symbol of resilience, courage, and the unbreakable spirit that defined their struggle in the face of overwhelming odds.

When the war finally ended, Smoky and Wynne returned to the United States, where she continued to bring joy and inspiration to those around her. She became a media sensation, appearing in newspapers, on television, and even in a few movies. Smoky's fame was not just a testament to her wartime service but also a celebration of the bond between humans and animals, a bond that had helped sustain the soldiers during the darkest days of the war.

Smoky lived a long and happy life after the war, passing away in 1957 at the age of 14. Her legacy, however, has lived on. In 2005, a life-size bronze statue of Smoky sitting in a GI helmet was unveiled in Cleveland, Ohio, where she and Wynne had made their home. The statue serves as a permanent tribute to Smoky's bravery and the incredible impact she had on the lives of those she touched.

Smoky's story is a powerful reminder that heroes come in all shapes and sizes. In a world dominated by conflict and destruction, a tiny Yorkshire Terrier managed to make a difference, not with brute strength or advanced weaponry, but with a courageous heart and a steadfast spirit. For the soldiers who knew her, Smoky was more than just a dog; she was a friend, a fellow soldier, and a beacon of hope in a time of darkness. And for the generations that followed, her story continues to inspire, showing that even the smallest among us can leave a lasting legacy of courage and kindness.

Wojtek the Bear: The Unlikely War Hero

Wojtek was no ordinary bear. His journey began in the spring of 1942, in the heat of World War II, when he was just a cub, barely strong enough to walk on his own. Found by a young boy in the mountainous region of Iran, Wojtek's life could have been one of solitude in the wild, but fate had other plans. The boy who found him knew he couldn't care for the cub on his own, so he brought Wojtek to a group of Polish soldiers who were part of the 22nd Artillery Supply Company of the Polish II Corps. These soldiers, who had been through the horrors of war and were far from their homes, took the little bear in, perhaps seeing in him a symbol of hope and innocence amidst the chaos surrounding them.

The soldiers fed Wojtek condensed milk from an empty vodka bottle, and he quickly became a beloved member of their unit. As Wojtek grew, so did his bond with the soldiers. He became their companion, their mascot, and eventually, something much more. Wojtek had a special talent for lifting the spirits of the men around him. Whether it was playfully wrestling with the soldiers, stealing their hats, or simply being his mischievous self, Wojtek brought joy to a group of men who desperately needed it. The soldiers treated him like one of their own, and Wojtek returned their affection with loyalty and a gentle nature that belied his growing size.

As time went on, Wojtek's role in the company became more than just that of a mascot. He was trained to carry heavy boxes of ammunition, a task that he took to with surprising ease. The sight of a bear carrying supplies alongside the soldiers became a common one, and Wojtek's fame began to spread among the Allied forces. But Wojtek was more than just a novelty; he was an essential part of the team. The soldiers would often rely on his strength and resilience during long, grueling marches, and Wojtek never failed them. His presence was a reminder that even in the darkest times, there could be moments of light, and that even the unlikeliest of heroes could emerge when they were needed most.

The bond between Wojtek and the soldiers was put to the ultimate test during the Battle of Monte Cassino, one of the most brutal and decisive battles of the Italian Campaign. The Polish II Corps played a crucial role in the Allied efforts to break through the German defenses, and Wojtek was right there with them. During the battle, Wojtek helped carry ammunition to the front lines, walking on his hind legs and holding the heavy shells in his arms, just like a human would. The sight of Wojtek calmly doing his part amidst the chaos of battle inspired the soldiers and became a symbol of their determination to overcome the odds.

Wojtek's contributions were so significant that he was officially enlisted as a soldier, complete with a rank and serial number. He became Private Wojtek, and the emblem of the 22nd Artillery Supply Company was changed to a depiction of a bear carrying an artillery shell, in honor of their most famous member. Wojtek's story spread far and wide, and he became a symbol of the indomitable spirit of the Polish soldiers and their fight for freedom.

After the war, Wojtek and his comrades were stationed in Scotland, where they were welcomed as heroes. Wojtek, however, was not just any hero—he was a bear, and his fame only grew. He would often appear at local events, delighting crowds with his playful antics and gentle nature. But as time passed, the soldiers who had been his family began to return to their homes, and Wojtek found himself alone once more. Understanding that Wojtek needed a new place to call home, the soldiers arranged for him to be transferred to Edinburgh Zoo, where he would live out the rest of his days.

At the zoo, Wojtek was well cared for, but he never forgot his comrades. Whenever Polish soldiers visited, Wojtek would stand up on his hind legs, just as he had done when carrying ammunition during the war. He would greet them with the same affection and recognition that he had shown in the battlefields of Italy. Wojtek's story continued to inspire those who heard it, reminding them of the bravery and resilience that can be found in even the most unlikely of heroes.

Wojtek passed away in 1963, but his legacy lives on. Statues and memorials have been erected in his honor in both Poland and Scotland, and his story is taught to children as a testament to the incredible bond between humans and animals, and the remarkable ways in which courage can manifest. Wojtek the Bear was more than just a soldier; he was a symbol of hope and friendship in a time of great darkness. His story teaches us that heroes come in all shapes and sizes, and that even in the midst of war, kindness, and courage can thrive.

The tale of Wojtek is one that resonates deeply, especially for young readers. It shows that bravery isn't always about fighting; sometimes, it's about carrying on, about helping those around you, and about being a source of strength for others. Wojtek's journey from a tiny cub in the mountains of Iran to a war hero recognized around the world is a story that continues to inspire, reminding us all of the extraordinary things that can happen when we care for one another, no matter the odds.

Chapter Three

Courage in the Skies

The Battle of Britain: The Young Pilots Who Defended the Skies

In the summer of 1940, the skies over Britain were filled with the roar of engines and the crackle of radio chatter as young pilots took to the air in one of the most critical battles of World War II. These were not seasoned veterans, but rather young men, many barely out of their teens, who were called upon to defend their country against an overwhelming enemy. This was the Battle of Britain, a fierce and heroic struggle where courage, determination, and the will to protect their homeland were the only things standing between Britain and the dark shadow of Nazi domination.

The story of the Battle of Britain is one of remarkable bravery. As the war raged across Europe, Adolf Hitler had turned his eyes toward Britain, intending to crush it under the weight of the Luftwaffe, Germany's powerful air force. Hitler's plan, known as Operation Sea Lion, was to invade Britain by first destroying its air defenses. If the Royal Air Force (RAF) could be defeated, nothing would stand in the way of German forces marching across the English countryside.

At the heart of this defense were the young pilots of the RAF, often referred to as "The Few" after a famous speech by Prime Minister Winston Churchill. These pilots came from diverse backgrounds, from city dwellers to farm boys, but they all shared a common goal: to protect their nation from invasion. Many of them had barely completed their training before being thrust into the cockpit of a Spitfire or Hurricane fighter plane, two of the most iconic aircraft of the war. The odds were heavily against them. The Luftwaffe had more planes, more experienced pilots, and greater resources. Yet what the RAF lacked in numbers, they made up for in sheer determination and the element of surprise.

Day after day, the skies over Britain became a deadly battleground. The young RAF pilots would scramble to their planes at the sound of the alarm, racing against time to intercept incoming German bombers. These aerial dogfights were intense, with planes twisting and turning at high speeds, bullets whizzing past as each pilot tried to outmaneuver the other. The stakes couldn't have been higher. A single mistake could mean death, not just for the pilot, but for the countless civilians below who depended on these young men to keep the enemy at bay.

Despite the overwhelming odds, the young pilots of the RAF quickly proved their mettle. Their knowledge of the local terrain, combined with the agility of their Spitfires and Hurricanes, allowed them to execute daring maneuvers that caught the Luftwaffe off guard. One of the most remarkable aspects of the Battle of Britain was the sense of camaraderie among the pilots. Though they were from different squadrons and backgrounds, they were united by a bond forged in the crucible of battle. Each mission could be their last, and this shared understanding created a deep sense of loyalty and friendship among the men.

The bravery of these pilots did not go unnoticed. On the ground, the people of Britain looked up to them as heroes. Stories began to circulate of their incredible feats—pilots who would continue to fight despite being outnumbered, who would land their damaged planes with barely any fuel left, and who would risk their lives to save a fellow pilot in distress. These stories provided hope and inspiration to a nation under siege, a reminder that no matter how dark the days seemed, there were still those willing to fight for freedom.

One of the most famous pilots of the Battle of Britain was Douglas Bader, a man who had lost both of his legs in a flying accident before the war. Refusing to be grounded, Bader returned to flying with the help of prosthetic legs and went on to become one of the most successful fighter aces of the battle. His story was a testament to the resilience and indomitable spirit that defined the RAF during this critical period.

As the summer turned to autumn, the intensity of the battle did not wane. The Luftwaffe shifted its tactics, launching night raids in an attempt to break Britain's resolve. Yet, the RAF continued to hold the line, adapting to the changing conditions and continuing to push back against the German assault. The turning point came in September 1940 when the Luftwaffe, frustrated by their inability to defeat the RAF, began targeting London and other major cities in what became known as the Blitz. This shift in strategy allowed the RAF to regroup and strengthen their defenses, ultimately leading to the failure of Hitler's plans to invade Britain.

The Battle of Britain officially ended in October 1940, with the Luftwaffe suffering significant losses and the invasion of Britain postponed indefinitely. The young pilots who had defended the skies over their homeland had not only protected Britain from invasion but had also delivered the first major defeat to Nazi Germany. Their courage and sacrifice became a symbol of resistance against tyranny and a source of inspiration for generations to come.

The impact of the Battle of Britain extended far beyond the immediate outcome of the war. It proved that Hitler's war machine was not invincible and that with determination, even a smaller force could stand up to a seemingly unstoppable enemy. The victory also boosted morale across the Allied nations, showing that the fight against fascism could be won.

For the young pilots, many of whom did not live to see the end of the war, their legacy is one of enduring heroism. They fought not for glory or recognition, but because they believed in the cause of freedom. Their story is a reminder that in times of great adversity, ordinary people can rise to extraordinary challenges and that even in the darkest of times, there is always hope.

As we remember these young men and their incredible deeds, we are reminded of the words of Winston Churchill, who famously said, "Never in the field of human conflict was so much owed by so many to so few." The young pilots of the Battle of Britain exemplified the very best of the human spirit, showing us all that courage, determination, and a commitment to what is right can change the course of history.

The Night Witches: The Fearless Female Pilots of WWII

During the dark and tumultuous years of World War II, a group of women took to the skies, defying stereotypes and shattering barriers. These women, known as the Night Witches, were part of the Soviet Union's 588th Night Bomber Regiment, and their story is one of courage, determination, and extraordinary skill. They flew through the night in flimsy planes, facing the enemy with an unyielding spirit that has become legendary. Their daring missions and unwavering resolve made them some of the most remarkable figures of WWII.

The Night Witches earned their fearsome nickname from the German soldiers they terrorized. The Germans, frustrated and frightened by the near-silent approach of these women pilots, described the sound of their planes as resembling the whooshing of a witch's broomstick in flight. The name stuck, and these female pilots embraced it with pride, knowing it embodied the fear they instilled in their enemies.

The 588th Night Bomber Regiment was formed in 1942, a time when the Soviet Union was desperately in need of every resource available to combat the Nazi invasion. Women had already begun to take on many roles traditionally held by men, but the idea of women serving in combat was still controversial. Despite this, Marina Raskova, a famous Soviet pilot and navigator, petitioned Stalin to allow the formation of an all-female aviation regiment. Stalin agreed, and Raskova was tasked with recruiting and training these young women.

The women who joined the Night Witches came from all walks of life. They were students, teachers, factory workers, and more, all united by a deep love for their country and a desire to protect it. Many were barely out of their teens, yet they were willing to face the dangers of war head-on. The rigorous training they underwent transformed them from civilians into skilled pilots and navigators. They learned to fly, navigate, and handle their aircraft with precision, often under the most challenging conditions.

The planes they flew were not the powerful war machines you might imagine. Instead, they piloted outdated Polikarpov Po-2 biplanes, which were originally designed for training and crop-dusting. These planes were slow, had no armor, and were made of wood and canvas. However, what they lacked in speed and protection, they made up for in agility and stealth. The Night Witches used these qualities to their advantage, flying close to the ground to avoid detection and turning off their engines as they approached their targets to glide in silently.

Their missions were perilous. The Night Witches would fly under the cover of darkness, carrying bombs to drop on enemy positions. They often flew multiple sorties in a single night, with each mission bringing new dangers. Anti-aircraft fire, enemy fighters, and the sheer challenge of navigating in the dark were constant threats. The cold was another enemy, as the open cockpits of their planes exposed them to freezing temperatures at high altitudes. Despite these challenges, the Night Witches displayed incredible bravery and determination.

One of the most remarkable aspects of the Night Witches' story is their success rate.

They flew over 23,000 missions and dropped more than 3,000 tons of bombs during the war. Their efforts significantly disrupted German operations, and their accuracy and persistence made them a formidable force. The Germans were so intimidated by the Night Witches that any soldier who downed one of their planes was automatically awarded the prestigious Iron Cross.

The Night Witches were not just fearless in the air; they also had to contend with the challenges of being women in a male-dominated military. They faced skepticism and doubt from some of their male counterparts, who questioned their abilities. Yet, these women proved themselves time and again, earning respect and admiration for their skill and dedication. They lived in harsh conditions, often sleeping outdoors or in makeshift tents, and their rations were meager. Despite this, their camaraderie and sense of purpose kept them going.

Many of the Night Witches became highly decorated heroes. Among them was Nadezhda Popova, one of the regiment's most famous pilots. She completed 852 missions and became a symbol of female bravery and resilience. Another was Yevdokiya Nikulina, who survived being shot down twice and continued to fly. Their stories, along with those of their comrades, are a testament to the incredible strength and determination of these women.

The legacy of the Night Witches extends far beyond their military achievements. They shattered gender norms and proved that women could be just as effective in combat as men. Their story continues to inspire people around the world, showing that courage knows no gender and that determination can overcome even the most daunting obstacles. They are remembered not just as pilots, but as pioneers who paved the way for future generations of women in aviation and the military.

For kids today, the story of the Night Witches is a powerful reminder of what can be achieved through bravery, teamwork, and a refusal to accept limitations. These women, flying their flimsy planes in the dead of night, remind us that heroism comes in many forms. Whether it's standing up for what's right, working together to achieve a common goal, or facing our fears head-on, the lessons from the Night Witches' story are timeless.

As we reflect on the remarkable feats of the Night Witches, it's important to remember that their story is just one of many incredible tales from World War II. The courage they displayed, the obstacles they overcame, and the impact they had on the war effort are all part of a larger narrative of bravery and sacrifice that shaped the course of history. Their story continues to inspire, offering valuable lessons in courage, resilience, and the power of the human spirit.

Chapter Five

Acts of Heroism

The Story of Oskar Schindler: The Man Who Saved Thousands

During one of the darkest times in human history, when the world was engulfed in the horrors of World War II, stories of unimaginable bravery and kindness emerged. Among these, the tale of Oskar Schindler stands out as a beacon of hope. Schindler was a man who, against all odds, risked everything to save thousands of lives. His story is not just a lesson in courage but a testament to the power of one person to make a difference in the face of overwhelming evil.

Oskar Schindler was born in 1908 in what was then Austria-Hungary, in a small town called Zwittau. He grew up in a time of great change, with the world around him shifting and evolving. As a young man, Schindler was known for his charm, business acumen, and ability to navigate complex situations. However, it was during the Second World War that he would truly find his place in history.

When the war broke out in 1939, Schindler, like many others, saw an opportunity. He joined the Nazi Party, not out of ideology but out of a desire to further his business interests. At first glance, he seemed like a man driven by self-interest, eager to profit from the chaos of war. He took over a factory in Kraków, Poland, where he employed Jewish workers. To the Nazis, these workers were cheap labor, but to Schindler, they would become much more.

As the war progressed, the situation for Jews in Nazi-occupied Europe became increasingly dire. The Nazis implemented their horrific "Final Solution," a plan to exterminate the Jewish population. Millions of Jews were rounded up, forced into ghettos, and sent to concentration camps where they faced unimaginable cruelty and death. It was in this environment of fear and despair that Oskar Schindler's conscience began to stir.

Schindler saw firsthand the brutality inflicted upon the Jewish people. He witnessed the liquidation of the Kraków Ghetto, where men, women, and children were torn from their homes and sent to die. He saw the inhumane conditions in the Plaszów concentration camp, where his factory workers were forced to live. These experiences had a profound effect on him, awakening a sense of responsibility and compassion that would drive his actions in the years to come.

Realizing the fate that awaited his Jewish workers, Schindler made a decision that would define his legacy. He resolved to protect as many Jews as he could, using his factory as a refuge. Schindler knew that as long as his workers were essential to the war effort, they would be spared from the death camps. So, he went to great lengths to ensure their safety, often at great personal risk.

Schindler's factory, which produced enamelware for the German military, became a sanctuary. He bribed Nazi officials, falsified documents, and used his considerable influence to keep his workers from being sent to their deaths. He argued that these workers were vital to the war effort, even when it was clear that they were not. His actions were not without risk; if he were caught, Schindler would likely have been executed for his defiance.

Despite the danger, Schindler continued his efforts. He spent vast sums of money, depleting his own fortune, to ensure the safety of his workers. He provided them with food, medical care, and other necessities, all while maintaining the façade of a loyal Nazi supporter. His actions were driven not by a desire for recognition or reward but by a deep sense of humanity and justice.

As the war neared its end and the Nazis began to lose power, Schindler's determination only grew stronger. In 1944, as the Red Army advanced toward Kraków, the Nazis ordered the evacuation of all factories and the liquidation of the remaining Jewish population. Schindler knew that this would mean certain death for his workers. In a final act of defiance, he convinced the authorities to allow him to move his factory and workers to Brünnlitz in Czechoslovakia, where they would be safe from the advancing Soviet forces.

This move was fraught with danger. Schindler had to bribe officials, navigate treacherous terrain, and ensure that his workers were not sent to the death camps during the relocation. But his efforts paid off. In Brünnlitz, he continued to protect his workers until the war ended in 1945. By that time, Oskar Schindler had saved the lives of over 1,200 Jews—men, women, and children who would have otherwise perished in the Holocaust.

After the war, Schindler's life took a different turn. He was no longer a wealthy businessman but a man who had spent everything to save others. He moved to Argentina, where he tried to start a new life, but he struggled with financial difficulties and health problems. Despite his hardships, the people he saved never forgot him. They considered him a hero, a man who had given them a second chance at life.

Oskar Schindler passed away in 1974, but his legacy lives on. He is buried in Jerusalem, where his grave is a site of pilgrimage for those who want to honor his memory. The people he saved and their descendants number in the thousands, a living testament to the impact of his actions.

The story of Oskar Schindler teaches us that even in the darkest times, there is always the possibility of light. It shows us that one person's actions, no matter how small they may seem, can have a profound impact on the lives of others. Schindler's bravery, compassion, and determination serve as an inspiration to us all, reminding us that we have the power to make a difference, even in the face of overwhelming odds.

For kids reading this story, Oskar Schindler is a reminder that heroes are not always those with the loudest voices or the most power. Sometimes, heroes are ordinary people who choose to do the right thing, even when it's difficult, dangerous, or unpopular. His story is a lesson in the importance of standing up for what is right, showing kindness and compassion, and using our abilities to help others. Through his example, we learn that the choices we make, even in the most challenging circumstances, can change the course of history and save lives.

The Little Ships of Dunkirk: A Miraculous Rescue

The story of the Little Ships of Dunkirk is one of the most miraculous and heartwarming tales to emerge from the dark days of World War II. It is a story of courage, unity, and the unbreakable spirit of ordinary people who came together to achieve the extraordinary. This incredible event took place during the early stages of the war, in the spring of 1940, when the fate of thousands of British and Allied soldiers hung in the balance.

In May 1940, the situation in Europe was dire. The German army, having swiftly overrun much of Western Europe, had cornered the British Expeditionary Force (BEF) and other Allied troops on the beaches of Dunkirk, a small town in northern France. Surrounded on all sides by the advancing German forces, the soldiers had no choice but to retreat to the coast, where they hoped to be evacuated across the English Channel to safety. However, the beaches of Dunkirk were shallow and not suited for large naval vessels, which meant that the evacuation seemed nearly impossible.

The British government, led by Prime Minister Winston Churchill, understood the gravity of the situation. If the BEF and the Allied troops were captured or killed, it would be a devastating blow to the war effort. The loss of these soldiers would have left Britain vulnerable to invasion, and the morale of the entire nation would have been shattered. The stakes could not have been higher.

In this desperate moment, a plan was hatched that would rely not on the might of the British Navy but on the bravery and selflessness of civilian volunteers. The government issued a call for help to the owners of small boats—fishing vessels, pleasure yachts, lifeboats, and even small motorboats—anything that could cross the Channel and reach the stranded soldiers on the beaches of Dunkirk. These vessels would become known as the "Little Ships."

The response to this call was nothing short of miraculous. From all over Britain, ordinary men and women, many of whom had never seen combat, answered the call. They knew the dangers they would face: the German Luftwaffe controlled the skies, and the waters were filled with mines and U-boats. But they also knew that they could not stand by while their fellow countrymen were in such desperate need.

On May 26, 1940, Operation Dynamo began. The Little Ships, numbering over 800, set out from the English coast and made their way across the Channel to Dunkirk. The sight of these tiny vessels braving the treacherous waters was both awe-inspiring and humbling. Some were manned by naval officers, but many were helmed by civilians—fishermen, ferry captains, and even weekend sailors—who had volunteered to take part in the rescue mission.

The conditions at Dunkirk were harrowing. The beaches were under constant bombardment from German artillery and aircraft. The soldiers, exhausted and demoralized, waited in long lines on the shore, hoping against hope that they would be rescued before it was too late. Many had lost their weapons and had only the clothes on their backs. The sight of the Little Ships approaching the beach must have seemed like a miracle.

Despite the danger, the Little Ships pressed on. They ferried soldiers from the beaches to the larger naval vessels waiting offshore, which could not get close enough to the shallow waters.

Some of the Little Ships made multiple trips, returning again and again to save as many lives as possible. The bravery of the volunteers knew no bounds. There are stories of men who refused to leave the beach until they had rescued as many soldiers as their boats could carry, even when it meant risking their own lives.

For nine days, the evacuation continued. The soldiers who were rescued were tired, hungry, and often wounded, but they were alive, thanks to the extraordinary efforts of the Little Ships and their crews. By the time Operation Dynamo was completed on June 4, 1940, over 338,000 soldiers had been evacuated from Dunkirk, far more than anyone had thought possible.

The success of the Dunkirk evacuation was a turning point in the war. It allowed the British Army to regroup and continue the fight against Nazi Germany. But more than that, it was a testament to the power of courage, determination, and the willingness of ordinary people to step up in times of crisis. The Little Ships of Dunkirk became a symbol of hope and resilience, showing that even in the darkest of times, there is light.

For the soldiers who were rescued, the memory of Dunkirk would stay with them for the rest of their lives. Many of them would go on to fight in other battles during the war, but they would never forget the sight of the Little Ships coming to their rescue when all hope seemed lost. The story of Dunkirk was a story they would tell their children and grandchildren, passing down the legacy of bravery and unity that defined that moment in history.

The legacy of the Little Ships lives on today. Every year, the Dunkirk Little Ships Association organizes commemorative events to honor those who took part in the evacuation. Many of the original vessels still exist, lovingly maintained and sailed by those who understand the importance of preserving this piece of history. These boats are more than just vessels—they are symbols of a time when ordinary people did extraordinary things.

The story of the Little Ships of Dunkirk is not just a story about World War II; it is a story about what it means to be human. It reminds us that in the face of overwhelming odds, we all have the capacity for courage, kindness, and selflessness. It is a story that continues to inspire and resonate, especially with young readers, who can learn from the example set by those brave souls who answered the call when their country needed them most.

Chapter Five

Unbreakable Bonds

The Friendship of Anne Frank and Hannah Goslar

Anne Frank and Hannah Goslar were more than just two girls growing up in the shadow of World War II; they were the best of friends. Their friendship, forged in the innocent days of childhood, became a beacon of light in one of history's darkest periods. Anne and Hannah's story is a powerful example of the endurance of the human spirit, the strength of friendship, and the resilience of hope, even when the world around them seemed to be falling apart.

The story begins in Amsterdam, a bustling city in the Netherlands, where Anne and Hannah first met. Both girls came from Jewish families who had fled Germany to escape the rise of Nazism. In Amsterdam, they found safety, for a time, and in each other, they found a kindred spirit. Anne and Hannah attended the same kindergarten, where they quickly became inseparable. They shared everything, from secrets and dreams to worries and fears, unaware of the storm that was gathering around them.

As they grew older, the bond between Anne and Hannah deepened. They played together after school, attended the same clubs, and even created their own games. Anne, with her lively imagination, loved to make up stories, while Hannah, a bit quieter, enjoyed listening to them. The two girls were different in many ways—Anne was outgoing and headstrong, while Hannah was more reserved and thoughtful—but their differences only seemed to draw them closer.

However, life in Amsterdam began to change as the war crept closer. The Nazis invaded the Netherlands in 1940, and soon, the persecution of Jews intensified. New laws were imposed that restricted Jewish life in the city. Jews could no longer attend public schools, visit parks, or even ride bicycles. Anne and Hannah, along with their families, were forced to wear yellow stars on their clothing, marking them as Jews. The two girls found themselves confined to their homes more and more, their world shrinking with each passing day.

Despite these challenges, Anne and Hannah's friendship remained steadfast. They continued to visit each other, finding comfort in their shared experiences. The Frank and Goslar families became even closer, often gathering for meals and discussions about the increasingly difficult situation. But as the Nazis tightened their grip on

Amsterdam, it became clear that things were going to get worse before they got better.

In 1942, when Anne was just 13 years old, the situation reached a critical point. The Frank family decided to go into hiding to escape the looming threat of deportation to Nazi concentration camps. Anne and her family moved into a secret annex behind her father's business, where they hoped to wait out the war in safety. Before they went into hiding, Anne said a tearful goodbye to Hannah, promising they would see each other again once the war was over.

For Anne, life in hiding was difficult. She missed the freedom of her previous life, and most of all, she missed her friends, especially

Hannah. During the long months in the annex, Anne kept a diary, pouring her thoughts and feelings onto the pages. In her diary, she often wrote about Hannah, remembering their happy times together and expressing her deep longing to see her friend again. Anne's diary would later become one of the most famous accounts of life during the Holocaust, but at the time, it was simply a way for her to cope with the isolation and fear that surrounded her.

Meanwhile, Hannah and her family were also facing increasing danger. In 1943, the Goslars were arrested by the Nazis and sent to the Westerbork transit camp, and later to the Bergen-Belsen concentration camp in Germany. Life in the camp was a nightmare. Food was scarce, disease was rampant, and the threat of death was ever-present. Yet, through it all, Hannah held on to the hope that she would one day be reunited with her friend Anne.

Remarkably, that hope was realized in early 1945, under the most unlikely of circumstances. By that time, Anne Frank had also been captured by the Nazis and was imprisoned in the same camp as Hannah—Bergen-Belsen. The camp was overcrowded, and the conditions were horrific. Hannah, who was in a slightly better part of the camp, learned through the grapevine that Anne was in the "star camp," a section for those considered unfit for work and awaiting deportation or worse.

Hannah's heart leaped at the possibility of seeing her friend again. She managed to sneak close to the barbed wire fence that separated their sections of the camp. Through the fence, the two friends communicated, throwing small packages of food and clothing over to Anne, who was weak and starving. Despite the terrible conditions and the ever-present threat of being caught, these brief encounters brought a flicker of joy to both girls. They were no longer alone; they had found each other again, even in the midst of unimaginable suffering.

Sadly, their reunion was short-lived. Just weeks before the camp was liberated by Allied forces, Anne Frank succumbed to the conditions in the camp and passed away. Hannah, however, survived the war. The loss of her dear friend was a wound that never fully healed, but Hannah carried Anne's memory with her for the rest of her life. She went on to tell the story of their friendship, ensuring that the world would never forget Anne Frank—not just as a symbol of the Holocaust, but as the lively, imaginative, and loving girl who was her best friend.

The friendship of Anne Frank and Hannah Goslar is a testament to the enduring power of human connection in even the darkest of times. It reminds us that even in the face of hatred and violence, the bonds of friendship and love can offer hope and strength. Through their story, Anne and Hannah continue to inspire young readers to believe in the power of friendship, to stand up for what is right, and to never lose hope, no matter how difficult life may seem.

The Brotherhood of the Tuskegee Airmen

In the heat of World War II, when the world was in turmoil and nations were desperate for heroes, a group of men rose to the challenge, not only to fight for their country but also to prove their worth in the face of overwhelming prejudice. These men were the Tuskegee Airmen, the first African-American military aviators in the United States Armed Forces. Their story is one of courage, determination, and brotherhood, a testament to the power of perseverance and the unbreakable bond of friendship.

The Tuskegee Airmen were born out of a time when racial segregation was deeply ingrained in American society. African-Americans were often denied opportunities to serve in the military, particularly in roles that required advanced training and skills, such as flying. Despite their desire to serve, black men were repeatedly told that they were not capable of becoming pilots, that they lacked the intelligence, skill, and courage necessary to fly combat missions. But these men refused to accept such limitations.

The journey of the Tuskegee Airmen began in 1941 at Tuskegee Institute in Alabama, where a group of young African-American men were selected to participate in an experimental program designed to train them as military pilots. It was a daunting task, as they were not only fighting to defend their country but also to prove that they deserved to be treated as equals. The training was grueling, pushing the men to their physical and mental limits. They faced not only the rigorous demands of learning to fly but also the constant sting of racism and discrimination. Many doubted their abilities, and some openly rooted for their failure.

Yet, these men forged ahead with a determination that was nothing short of extraordinary. They knew that their success would pave the way for future generations of African-Americans, not just in the military, but in all walks of life. The bond between the trainees quickly grew strong, as they realized that they could only succeed by supporting one another. They became more than just comrades; they became brothers.

Their training culminated in the formation of the 99th Fighter Squadron, the first

African-American fighter squadron in the U.S. Army Air Corps. In 1943, the squadron was deployed to North Africa, where they flew combat missions in the skies over the Mediterranean and Europe. These missions were perilous, with enemy aircraft and anti-aircraft fire posing constant threats. But the Tuskegee Airmen proved their worth time and again, escorting bombers on dangerous missions deep into enemy territory and engaging in dogfights with German planes.

Their performance was exemplary. The Tuskegee Airmen earned a reputation for their skill and bravery, and the bomber crews they escorted quickly came to trust and respect them. Despite the dangers, the Tuskegee Airmen had one of the lowest loss rates of any escort fighter group during the war. Their success in the air was a direct result of their intense training, teamwork, and the unbreakable bond they shared.

But their battle was not only in the skies. On the ground, they continued to face discrimination, even from their fellow soldiers. They were often relegated to inferior facilities and denied the same privileges as their white counterparts. Yet, they carried themselves with dignity and grace, knowing that their actions spoke louder than any words. They understood that they were not just fighting for victory in the war, but for the future of their race and their country.

The Tuskegee Airmen's bravery and determination did not go unnoticed. By the end of the war, they had flown over 1,500 missions, destroyed or damaged 409 enemy aircraft, and received numerous honors, including Distinguished Flying Crosses, Bronze Stars, and Silver Stars. Their achievements were a powerful statement against the racism and prejudice that had sought to keep them grounded.

The legacy of the Tuskegee Airmen extends far beyond their wartime accomplishments. They shattered stereotypes and paved the way for the integration of the U.S. military. In 1948, just three years after the war ended, President Harry S. Truman signed Executive Order 9981, which desegregated the armed forces, largely due to the outstanding performance of the Tuskegee

Airmen and other African-American service members during the war.

But perhaps their most lasting legacy is the inspiration they provided to future generations. The story of the Tuskegee Airmen is a story of overcoming obstacles, of refusing to accept limitations, and of standing together in the face of adversity. It is a story that teaches us that true courage is not just about facing external dangers, but about confronting and overcoming the prejudices and injustices of the world around us.

For the children who read about the Tuskegee Airmen, their story is a reminder that greatness is not determined by the color of one's skin, but by the content of one's character and the strength of one's resolve. The Tuskegee Airmen showed that with determination, skill, and, above all, brotherhood, anything is possible. They proved that even in the darkest times, there is always room for light, and that true heroes can come from the most unexpected places.

The bond between the Tuskegee Airmen was forged in the crucible of war, but it was tempered by their shared struggle against discrimination and their unwavering commitment to one another. They were more than just a group of pilots; they were a symbol of hope, of what could be achieved when people refuse to let hatred and prejudice define them. Their story continues to inspire and remind us that the fight for equality and justice is a battle worth fighting, and that true victory comes when we stand together as one.

As we remember the Tuskegee Airmen, we honor not just their achievements in the skies, but the enduring spirit of brotherhood and resilience that carried them through the toughest of times. Their legacy is a beacon of hope for all who dare to dream of a better, more just world, where every person is judged not by their race or background, but by the content of their character and the courage of their convictions.

Chapter Six

Resistance Fighters

The French Resistance: Ordinary People Doing Extraordinary Things

During World War II, the world saw the rise of many heroes, some in uniform and others in ordinary clothes, whose bravery shaped the course of history. One of the most inspiring examples of courage and resilience came from the French Resistance—a group of everyday citizens who stood up against the occupying Nazi forces in France. These were not soldiers by profession; they were teachers, farmers, shopkeepers, students, and even children. Yet, their determination to fight for freedom made them extraordinary figures in the story of World War II.

The French Resistance began in the shadows, sparked by the German invasion of France in 1940. The Nazis quickly took control of much of the country, establishing a regime that oppressed the French people and sought to eradicate their way of life. But the spirit of resistance could not be extinguished. It flickered to life in the hearts of those who refused to accept the tyranny imposed upon them. These brave souls understood that their fight was not just for themselves but for the future of their nation and the principles of liberty and justice.

At first, the Resistance was small, a collection of isolated groups working independently to disrupt the Nazi occupation. These early resisters engaged in acts of sabotage, such as derailing trains carrying German supplies, cutting communication lines, and distributing anti-Nazi propaganda. They knew that their actions, though small in scale, could have a significant impact on the morale of both the occupiers and the occupied. Even the smallest act of defiance was a beacon of hope for those living under the brutal regime.

One of the most remarkable aspects of the French Resistance was the way it united people from all walks of life. In a time when division could have easily taken root, the Resistance brought together men and women, young and old, from all social classes and political beliefs. The common goal of liberating France transcended differences, creating a powerful network of allies. Farmers who knew the countryside like the back of their hand guided Resistance fighters through secret paths, while students used their knowledge of the city streets to evade German patrols. Women played a crucial role as well, often underestimated by the Nazis, they served as couriers, spies, and even leaders of Resistance cells.

The risks taken by these ordinary people were immense. The Nazi regime was ruthless, and the penalties for being caught as a member of the Resistance were severe. Many were arrested, tortured, or executed, yet this did not deter others from joining the cause. The courage of the Resistance fighters was not only in their willingness to face danger but also in their ability to keep hope alive in the darkest of times. They understood that every act of defiance, no matter how small, was a step towards freedom.

One of the most famous members of the French Resistance was Jean Moulin, a former civil servant who became a symbol of the movement. Appointed by General Charles de Gaulle to unite the various Resistance groups under a single command, Moulin traveled across France, risking his life to bring unity to the fragmented Resistance. He knew that only by working together could the Resistance achieve its ultimate goal of liberating France. Moulin's work was instrumental in organizing the Maquis—rural guerrilla bands that played a vital role in harassing German forces and gathering intelligence for the Allies.

The Maquis fighters were often young men who had fled to the countryside to avoid being conscripted into forced labor by the Nazis. Living in the forests and mountains, they carried out daring raids on German convoys, ambushed patrols, and sabotaged supply lines. Despite being outgunned and outnumbered, their knowledge of the terrain and their unbreakable spirit made them formidable opponents. Their efforts were crucial in weakening German control in the lead-up to the Allied invasion of Normandy, known as D-Day.

The role of the French Resistance in supporting the D-Day invasion cannot be overstated. As the Allies prepared to land on the beaches of Normandy in June 1944, the Resistance intensified their efforts to disrupt German communications and transportation networks. They blew up bridges, cut telephone wires, and provided vital intelligence to the Allied forces. These actions delayed German reinforcements and contributed significantly to the success of the invasion, which marked the beginning of the end for Nazi occupation in Western Europe.

The bravery of the French Resistance fighters did not go unnoticed by the world. Their actions inspired others living under occupation to resist and provided a beacon of hope that the Nazi regime could be defeated. After the war, many of these ordinary heroes returned to their previous lives, often without recognition or reward. They had not fought for glory or accolades, but for the simple yet profound belief in freedom and justice. Their legacy is a testament to the power of ordinary people to do extraordinary things when faced with extraordinary circumstances.

The story of the French Resistance is not just a tale of bravery during World War II; it is a reminder that the strength of a nation lies in its people. It shows that even in the face of overwhelming odds, courage, unity, and determination can prevail. For the children reading this, the story of the French Resistance is a lesson in the importance of standing up for what is right, even when it is difficult or dangerous. It teaches us that we all have the potential to be heroes in our own way, by helping others, standing against injustice, and never giving up hope.

The French Resistance fighters may have been ordinary people, but their actions were nothing short of extraordinary. Their courage helped to free a nation and left a lasting legacy of what can be achieved when people come together for a just cause. The story of their resistance during World War II is one that continues to inspire, showing that even in the darkest times, there is always light to be found in the bravery of those who refuse to be conquered.

The Polish Underground: Fighting Back Against the Nazis

During World War II, the world witnessed incredible acts of bravery and resilience. Among the many stories of resistance, few are as inspiring as the tale of the Polish Underground.

When Poland was invaded by Nazi Germany in 1939, the country found itself under the brutal occupation of one of the most powerful and ruthless military forces in history. But instead of succumbing to despair, ordinary Poles chose to fight back, forming one of the most remarkable resistance movements of the war: the Polish Underground.

The Polish Underground, also known as the Home Army (Armia Krajowa), was a secret organization composed of men, women, and even children who refused to accept the Nazi occupation of their homeland. This underground army wasn't just a group of soldiers; it included people from all walks of life—teachers, doctors, farmers, students, and workers—who risked everything to fight for their country's freedom.

They knew that if they were caught, they would face imprisonment, torture, or even death, but their determination to free Poland from Nazi tyranny was stronger than their fear.

Operating in the shadows, the Polish Underground became a formidable force against the Nazis. They engaged in a wide range of activities, from gathering intelligence and spreading propaganda to sabotaging German supply lines and conducting guerrilla warfare. The underground members worked tirelessly to disrupt Nazi operations, often at great personal risk. One of the most effective tactics they used was sabotage. Members of the underground would derail trains, blow up bridges, and destroy key infrastructure to hinder the Nazi war effort. These acts of sabotage were carefully planned and executed with precision, often involving months of preparation and coordination. The goal was to create as much disruption as possible without being detected by the German forces.

But the Polish Underground wasn't just about sabotage and warfare; it was also about maintaining hope and morale among the Polish people. During the occupation, the Nazis sought to crush the spirit of the Polish nation, banning newspapers, books, and any form of cultural expression that did not align with their ideology. In response, the underground established a secret press that produced newspapers, leaflets, and books to keep the Polish culture and spirit alive. These publications were distributed in secret, often at great personal risk, and they played a crucial role in keeping the Polish people informed and motivated to resist.

One of the most remarkable aspects of the Polish Underground was its network of couriers. These brave men and women, often disguised as ordinary civilians, carried vital information, weapons, and supplies between different units of the underground. The couriers operated under constant threat, knowing that capture by the Nazis would mean certain death. Yet, they continued their work with unwavering determination, ensuring that the underground remained connected and effective.

The Polish Underground also played a significant role in helping Jewish people escape from the Nazis. In the face of the Holocaust, where millions of Jews were being rounded up and sent to concentration camps, the underground established routes for smuggling Jews out of the ghettos and providing them with false documents and safe houses. Many members of the underground paid the ultimate price for their efforts, but their bravery saved countless lives.

One of the most dramatic moments in the history of the Polish Underground was the Warsaw Uprising of 1944. After years of preparation, the underground launched a full-scale rebellion against the Nazi occupiers in Warsaw, the capital of Poland. For 63 days, the fighters of the underground, along with civilians, battled the Nazis in the streets of Warsaw. Despite being vastly outnumbered and outgunned, they fought with incredible courage and determination. The uprising was ultimately crushed by the Nazis, and the city of Warsaw was left in ruins. However, the bravery of those who fought in the uprising became a symbol of the indomitable spirit of the Polish people and their unwavering desire for freedom.

The story of the Polish Underground is one of incredible heroism and resilience. These brave men and women showed the world that even in the darkest of times, ordinary people could come together to do extraordinary things. They fought not just for their own freedom, but for the freedom of others, risking everything to stand up against tyranny and oppression.

For young readers, the story of the Polish Underground is a powerful reminder that courage comes in many forms. It is not just about fighting on the battlefield; it is about standing up for what is right, even when the odds are against you. The members of the Polish Underground demonstrated that true bravery is about helping others, protecting the innocent, and never giving up hope, no matter how difficult the circumstances.

Their legacy lives on as an example of the strength of the human spirit and the importance of fighting for justice and freedom. The Polish Underground may have operated in the shadows, but their story continues to shine as a beacon of inspiration for generations to come. They remind us that even in the face of overwhelming adversity, we have the power to make a difference and change the course of history.

In learning about the Polish Underground, young readers can find inspiration in the courage and determination of those who came before them. They can see that bravery is not about being fearless, but about facing fear and choosing to act despite it. The story of the Polish Underground is not just a story of war; it is a story of hope, of resilience, and of the unbreakable bonds that unite people in the pursuit of a common cause. It is a story that teaches us all about the power of ordinary people to do extraordinary things, and it is a story that deserves to be remembered and passed down through the generations.

Chapter Seven

Brave Young Souls

The Story of Anne Frank: A Young Girl's Diary of Hope

Anne Frank's story is one of the most poignant and powerful narratives to emerge from the darkness of World War II. Her diary, kept during the two years she and her family spent hiding from the Nazis, provides a unique and deeply personal glimpse into the life of a young Jewish girl during one of history's darkest periods. Anne's story is not just a tale of war and persecution, but a testament to the resilience of the human spirit, the power of hope, and the enduring strength of a young girl's voice in the face of unimaginable adversity.

Anne Frank was born on June 12, 1929, in Frankfurt, Germany, to Otto and Edith Frank. Anne, along with her older sister Margot, grew up in a warm and loving household. However, their peaceful life was shattered when Adolf Hitler and the Nazi Party rose to power in Germany. The Franks, like many Jewish families, faced increasing persecution under the Nazi regime. Hoping to escape the growing danger, the family relocated to Amsterdam in 1933, where Otto Frank established a successful business and the family settled into their new life.

However, the safety they sought was short-lived. In May 1940, Nazi Germany invaded the Netherlands, and soon, the lives of the Jewish population in Amsterdam were thrown into turmoil. As the Nazi grip tightened, Jews were subjected to increasingly oppressive laws and restrictions. For Anne, this meant no longer being able to attend her school, play with her non-Jewish friends, or even go to certain places in the city. Life became a daily struggle to navigate a world where fear and uncertainty reigned.

As the situation grew more dangerous, Otto Frank made the difficult decision to move his family into hiding. On July 6, 1942, the Frank family, along with four other Jewish refugees—the Van Pels family and Fritz Pfeffer—went into hiding in a secret annex located behind Otto's business office. The entrance to the annex was concealed by a bookcase, providing a hidden sanctuary where they would live in constant fear of discovery for the next two years.

It was during this time that Anne began to write in the diary she had received as a gift on her 13th birthday, just weeks before going into hiding. This diary, which she named "Kitty," became Anne's closest confidante. In its pages, she poured out her thoughts, fears, hopes, and dreams. Anne wrote about the mundane details of daily life in the annex—the cramped quarters, the tension among the inhabitants, and the constant threat of being discovered by the Nazis.

But Anne's diary is much more than a record of the hardships of life in hiding. It is a profound and moving exploration of a young girl's inner world. Despite the terror that surrounded her, Anne never lost her sense of curiosity, her love of life, or her desire to understand the world around her. She wrote with remarkable insight about the complexities of human nature, the cruelty of war, and her longing for freedom and normalcy.

Anne's diary also reveals her growth as a writer. As time went on, her entries became more reflective and mature. She grappled with her identity, her relationship with her parents, and her feelings of isolation. Anne dreamt of becoming a famous writer or journalist, and she hoped that one day her diary would be published as a record of what she and millions of others endured during the war. She believed that through her writing, she could make a difference in the world, even if she was trapped in the annex.

Throughout her time in hiding, Anne clung to her optimism and her belief in the goodness of people, despite the horrors she knew were happening outside the annex walls. "In spite of everything," she wrote, "I still believe that people are really good at heart." This belief is one of the most enduring aspects of Anne's story—it is a message of hope that continues to resonate with readers around the world.

However, Anne's story took a tragic turn on August 4, 1944, when the annex was raided by the Gestapo, the Nazi secret police. The Franks, along with the other inhabitants of the annex, were arrested and deported to concentration camps. Anne and her sister Margot were eventually sent to the Bergen-Belsen concentration camp in Germany, where they both succumbed to typhus in March 1945, just weeks before the camp was liberated by Allied forces.

Anne Frank's diary was found by Miep Gies, one of the Dutch citizens who had helped the Frank family during their time in hiding. Miep preserved the diary, and after the war, she gave it to Otto Frank, the only surviving member of the Frank family. Otto made the difficult decision to fulfill Anne's wish of becoming a writer by having her diary published. In 1947, "The Diary of a Young Girl" was first published in Dutch, and it has since been translated into more than

70 languages, touching the hearts of millions of readers around the world.

Anne Frank's diary is more than just a historical document; it is a powerful reminder of the horrors of war and the strength of the human spirit. Through her words, Anne has become a symbol of the innocent lives lost during the Holocaust, but she has also become a symbol of hope, resilience, and the enduring power of a single voice. Her story continues to inspire generations of readers, reminding us all of the importance of tolerance, understanding, and the need to stand up against injustice.

Even though Anne Frank's life was tragically cut short, her words live on, offering us a window into the experiences of those who lived through one of the darkest periods in history. Her diary is a testament to the idea that even in the face of overwhelming darkness, the light of the human spirit can still shine brightly. Anne Frank's legacy is one of courage, compassion, and an unshakable belief in the goodness of humanity—a legacy that will continue to inspire and educate for generations to come.

The Kindertransport: Saving Jewish Children from the Holocaust

The story of the Kindertransport is one of courage, sacrifice, and hope during one of the darkest periods in history. As World War II loomed and the Nazi regime intensified its persecution of Jews, a remarkable effort was undertaken to save as many Jewish children as possible from the horrors that awaited them. The Kindertransport, which means "Children's Transport" in German, was a daring mission that brought thousands of Jewish children to safety, far from the reach of the Nazis.

In the late 1930s, life for Jewish families in Germany, Austria, Czechoslovakia, and other parts of Europe became increasingly perilous. The rise of Adolf Hitler and his hateful ideology meant that Jews were no longer safe in their own homes. Anti-Semitic laws stripped Jewish people of their rights, while violent attacks, such as the infamous Kristallnacht or "Night of Broken Glass," left Jewish communities in terror. During this night in November 1938, synagogues were burned, Jewish businesses were destroyed, and many Jewish people were arrested or killed. It was a clear signal to the world that the situation was dire and that something had to be done.

As the threat of war became imminent, a group of concerned individuals and organizations in Britain recognized the need to act quickly. They realized that while it might not be possible to save entire families, there might still be a way to save the children. With the support of the British government, a plan was devised to bring Jewish children to safety in the United Kingdom. This operation became known as the Kindertransport.

The Kindertransport was a massive undertaking, involving the coordination of many different people, including Jewish and non-Jewish volunteers, religious leaders, and government officials. The plan was simple yet heart-wrenching: Jewish parents would send their children to Britain, knowing that it might be the last time they would ever see them. These children, most of whom were between the ages of five and seventeen, were selected based on their vulnerability and the willingness of British families to take them in.

The process began with the identification and registration of children in need. Jewish organizations in Europe worked tirelessly to compile lists of children who could be saved. Parents had to make the agonizing decision to send their children away, knowing that they would be left behind in a land where their safety could no longer be guaranteed. It was an unimaginable act of love and courage, driven by the desperate hope that their children would have a chance to survive and build a future, even if it meant doing so far from home.

Once selected, the children were gathered at designated departure points, usually railway stations. Saying goodbye to their parents was an emotional and painful experience. For many children, these moments would be their last memories of their families. The trains, often crowded and filled with nervous chatter, carried the children through countries in turmoil. The journey to safety was long and uncertain, but the children knew they were heading toward a place where they would be safe.

When the Kindertransport trains arrived in Britain, the children were met by volunteers and foster families who had agreed to care for them. Some children were taken in by relatives, while others were placed with strangers who opened their homes and hearts to them. These British families played a crucial role in the success of the Kindertransport, providing not only shelter but also a sense of belonging to children who had been torn from everything they knew.

Life in Britain was a mix of relief and adjustment for the Kindertransport children. They were safe from the immediate danger of the Nazis, but the trauma of separation from their families and the uncertainty of what had happened to their loved ones weighed heavily on them. Many of the children did not speak English and had to adapt to a new culture and way of life. Despite these challenges, the children displayed remarkable resilience. They attended school, made new friends, and tried to build a sense of normalcy in their new lives.

The impact of the Kindertransport was profound. Between 1938 and 1940, approximately 10,000 Jewish children were brought to safety in Britain. While this was a significant achievement, it was also a bittersweet victory. The children who were saved through the Kindertransport had been given a chance at life, but the fate of their families remained uncertain. As the war progressed and news of the Holocaust began to spread, many of the Kindertransport children learned that their parents and relatives had been killed in concentration camps. The pain of this loss was unimaginable, and many of the children carried this grief with them for the rest of their lives.

Despite the sorrow and loss, the Kindertransport remains a testament to the power of human compassion and the courage of those who took action in the face of evil. The people who organized the Kindertransport, the families who took in the children, and the children themselves—all played a role in one of the most remarkable rescue missions of World War II. Their stories serve as a reminder that even in the darkest of times, there are always those who will stand up for what is right and fight to protect the innocent.

The legacy of the Kindertransport lives on today. Many of the children who were saved went on to lead successful lives, contributing to society in countless ways. They became doctors, teachers, artists, and leaders, carrying with them the lessons of their past and the knowledge that they were part of something extraordinary. The Kindertransport also serves as a powerful example of the importance of helping those in need, regardless of the risks or challenges involved.

For young readers today, the story of the Kindertransport is not just a history lesson; it is an inspiring tale of bravery, kindness, and hope. It shows that even in the face of overwhelming danger, people can come together to do what is right. The Kindertransport is a story of survival, but it is also a story of humanity at its best. It reminds us that the actions of a few can make a difference in the lives of many and that even in the darkest moments, there is always hope.

Chapter Eight

Hidden Heroes

Irena Sendler: The Woman Who Saved 2,500 Children

Irena Sendler was a woman whose courage and determination shone brightly in the darkest days of World War II. Her story is one of remarkable bravery, compassion, and an unyielding commitment to saving innocent lives. In the midst of the Nazi occupation of Poland, Irena became a beacon of hope for thousands of Jewish children, risking her own life to protect theirs.

Born in 1910 in Warsaw, Poland, Irena grew up with a strong sense of social justice, instilled in her by her father, who was a doctor. Her father passed away when she was just seven years old, but his influence lived on in her. He had taught her that everyone, regardless of their background or beliefs, deserved to be treated with kindness and respect. This lesson would guide Irena throughout her life, especially during the war.

When World War II broke out in 1939, Irena was working as a social worker in Warsaw. The city quickly fell under Nazi control, and life for the Jewish population became increasingly perilous. The Nazis established the Warsaw Ghetto, confining hundreds of thousands of Jews within its walls, subjecting them to starvation, disease, and brutal treatment. The conditions in the ghetto were horrific, and it became clear to Irena that something had to be done.

Determined to help, Irena joined the Polish underground resistance movement, Zegota, which was dedicated to aiding Jews during the Holocaust. Using her position as a social worker, she gained access to the ghetto, ostensibly to check on the health and welfare of the inhabitants. In reality, she was part of a covert operation to rescue Jewish children from certain death.

Irena and her team of helpers devised numerous ingenious methods to smuggle children out of the ghetto. They used anything they could to hide the children: toolboxes, sacks, and even coffins. Sometimes, Irena would take a child out under the cover of darkness, hidden in her coat. Other times, she would sedate infants and place them in small boxes or bags, passing them off as ordinary parcels. It was a dangerous game; if caught, Irena and the children she was trying to save would have faced execution.

But Irena was not deterred. She was driven by a fierce determination to save as many lives as possible. Each child she rescued was placed with a Polish family, a convent, or an orphanage, where they would be safe from the Nazis. However, she knew that these children needed more than just physical safety; they needed to retain their identities and have a chance to reunite with their families after the war. To ensure this, Irena meticulously recorded the names and details of each child she saved, writing them on slips of paper that she hid in jars and buried in a neighbor's garden. She hoped that one day, when the war was over, these children could be reunited with their parents or at least know their true heritage.

As the war dragged on, the risks grew greater. The Nazis were determined to crush the resistance, and anyone caught helping Jews faced severe punishment. In 1943, Irena's luck ran out. She was arrested by the Gestapo and brutally tortured, but she refused to betray her comrades or the children she had saved. Despite the relentless interrogation and the unimaginable pain she endured, Irena remained silent.

Sentenced to death, Irena faced the firing squad with the same courage that had driven her throughout the war. But fate intervened. Members of the Polish resistance managed to bribe a German officer, and on the day of her execution, Irena was secretly released. The Gestapo announced her death, and Irena went into hiding, continuing her work under a false identity.

By the end of the war, Irena had saved around 2,500 Jewish children, more than almost any other individual during the Holocaust. Despite her incredible achievements, Irena never saw herself as a hero. She believed that she had simply done what was right, what was necessary in a time of unimaginable evil. She once said, "I was brought up to believe that a person must be rescued when drowning, regardless of religion and nationality."

Irena's story did not end with the war. She lived to see many of the children she saved grow up and lead full lives, though tragically, many of their families had perished in the Holocaust. After the war, she continued her work in social services, dedicating her life to helping those in need. For decades, her story remained relatively unknown outside of Poland, but in the later years of her life, she received international recognition for her extraordinary courage.

In 1965, Irena Sendler was recognized by Yad Vashem as one of the Righteous Among the Nations, an honor given to non-Jews who risked their lives to save Jews during the Holocaust. She also received numerous other awards, including Poland's highest honor, the Order of the White Eagle. However, she remained humble about her accomplishments, insisting that she had only done what any decent person would have done in her situation.

Irena Sendler passed away in 2008 at the age of 98, leaving behind a legacy of bravery, compassion, and unwavering moral strength. Her story is a powerful reminder of the impact that one person can have, even in the face of overwhelming adversity. Irena's life teaches us that courage is not the absence of fear but the determination to act in spite of it. Her actions during World War II saved thousands of lives and continue to inspire generations to stand up against injustice, no matter the cost.

For young readers today, Irena Sendler's story is not just a tale of heroism; it's a lesson in the power of empathy, the importance of standing up for what is right, and the difference that one person can make in the world. In a time when the world was engulfed in hatred and violence, Irena Sendler chose to be a beacon of hope and humanity, proving that even in the darkest of times, goodness can prevail.

Nicholas Winton: The British "Schindler"

During the dark and tumultuous years of World War II, countless lives were at risk, especially those of Jewish children. The Nazis' relentless persecution left millions in danger, with few places to turn for refuge. In the midst of this chaos, one man quietly stepped forward to make a difference. Nicholas Winton, a British stockbroker, became a beacon of hope for hundreds of children who faced the terrifying reality of the Holocaust. His story, often compared to that of Oskar Schindler, is a testament to the extraordinary courage, compassion, and determination of one man to make a difference in a world seemingly devoid of hope.

Nicholas Winton's story began in December 1938, just a few months before the outbreak of World War II. Winton had planned to spend his Christmas holiday in Switzerland, but a last-minute change of plans led him to Prague, Czechoslovakia. His friend, Martin Blake, who was working with Jewish refugees in the country, urged Winton to visit Prague and witness the dire situation firsthand. What Winton saw in Prague shocked him to his core. The city was overflowing with Jewish refugees, mostly children, who had fled from the Sudetenland after it was annexed by Nazi Germany. These children were facing an uncertain future, and the prospects of escape were growing dimmer by the day.

Moved by the plight of these children, Winton quickly realized that something had to be done to save them. With no experience in refugee work or international politics, Winton took it upon himself to organize a rescue operation. His mission was clear: to find a way to get as many children as possible out of Czechoslovakia and into safe countries before it was too late. Winton's first challenge was to secure the necessary permits and visas to allow the children to enter other countries. This was no small task, as most countries were reluctant to accept Jewish refugees at the time. Winton focused his efforts on Britain, where he believed he had the best chance of success. He worked tirelessly, contacting governments, embassies, and even the British Home Office to secure the documents needed for the children's safe passage.

In addition to the legal hurdles, Winton faced the daunting task of raising funds to cover the costs of the rescue operation. Each child required a £50 guarantee, a significant sum at the time, to ensure that they would not become a financial burden on the British government. Undeterred by the challenges, Winton began to raise money through donations, appealing to friends, family, and even strangers for help. He also set up an office in Prague, where he and a small team of volunteers worked around the clock to process applications, secure transportation, and make arrangements for the children's care once they arrived in Britain.

Winton's efforts were nothing short of heroic. Between March and August 1939, he organized eight trains, known as Kindertransport, which carried 669 children from Prague to safety in Britain. These trains were a lifeline for the children, who faced an uncertain fate if they remained in Nazi-occupied Europe. The journey was long and perilous, often taking days to complete. The children, many of whom were separated from their parents for the first time, displayed remarkable bravery as they embarked on this life-changing journey to an unknown land.

Upon their arrival in Britain, the children were placed with foster families, who had volunteered to care for them. Winton personally oversaw the placement of each child, ensuring that they were well cared for and had the opportunity to rebuild their lives. He maintained contact with many of the children, following their progress as they adapted to their new homes and, in many cases, thrived in their new environment.

Despite his incredible efforts, Winton's work went largely unrecognized for many years. He never sought recognition or praise for his actions, viewing his work as simply the right thing to do. It wasn't until 1988, nearly 50 years after the rescue operation, that Winton's remarkable story came to light. A chance discovery by his wife, Greta, of an old scrapbook in their attic revealed the full extent of his efforts. The scrapbook contained lists of the children he had saved, along with photographs, letters, and documents detailing the rescue operation. Greta brought the scrapbook to the attention of a journalist, and soon after, Winton's story began to receive the recognition it so richly deserved.

In 1988, Winton was invited to appear on the BBC television program "That's Life!" where he was reunited with several of the children he had saved, now grown adults. It was an emotional and heartwarming moment, as the children, who had never forgotten the man who saved their lives, embraced him and expressed their gratitude. The program brought Winton's story to the public's attention, and he quickly became known as the "British Schindler," a reference to Oskar Schindler, who saved more than a thousand Jews during the Holocaust.

Winton's legacy is one of quiet heroism and unwavering commitment to doing what is right, even in the face of overwhelming odds. His story serves as a powerful reminder of the impact that one person can have, even in the darkest of times. The 669 children he saved went on to lead full and productive lives, with many becoming doctors, teachers, and professionals who contributed to society in countless ways. They, in turn, raised families of their own, ensuring that Winton's legacy would live on through future generations.

Nicholas Winton was knighted by Queen Elizabeth II in 2003 in recognition of his extraordinary humanitarian efforts. He continued to speak about his experiences well into his later years, always emphasizing the importance of taking action to help others, regardless of the challenges. Winton passed away in 2015 at the age of 106, leaving behind a legacy of compassion, courage, and kindness that continues to inspire people around the world.

In a world that often seems filled with division and conflict, Nicholas Winton's story reminds us of the incredible difference that one person can make. His actions, driven by a deep sense of empathy and moral responsibility, saved hundreds of lives and provided a beacon of hope in one of history's darkest chapters. As young readers learn about his story, they are reminded that even in the face of overwhelming adversity, there is always the possibility to make a positive difference in the lives of others.

Chapter Nine

Allies from Afar

The Navajo Code Talkers: The Secret Weapon

During World War II, the United States faced a formidable challenge: how to communicate securely in a way that the enemy could not intercept or decipher. This was a time when radios were essential for sending orders and coordinating troops, but these transmissions were often intercepted by enemy forces. The risk was high; if the enemy could decode the messages, entire operations could be compromised, and countless lives could be lost. The need for a secure, unbreakable code was more urgent than ever.

Enter the Navajo Code Talkers—a group of Native American Marines whose extraordinary contribution became one of the most unique and successful operations in military history. These men used their native language, Navajo, to develop a code that played a crucial role in the Pacific Theater of World War II, helping to turn the tide in favor of the Allied forces.

The idea of using Native American languages as a code wasn't entirely new. In World War I, Choctaw soldiers had been used similarly, but World War II presented a more significant challenge. By 1942, the Japanese military had proven itself highly skilled in code-breaking. They had broken every American code used up until that point. Something different was needed—something entirely new.

Philip Johnston, a civil engineer and World War I veteran, was the man behind the idea of using the Navajo language. He was one of the few non-Navajos who spoke the language fluently, having grown up on a Navajo reservation as the son of a missionary. Johnston knew that Navajo was an incredibly complex and unwritten language, spoken only by the Navajo people. It was a language so difficult and unique that it could serve as the perfect foundation for an unbreakable code.

Johnston approached the U.S. Marine Corps with his idea in early 1942. Initially, military officials were skeptical. However, a demonstration quickly convinced them of the plan's potential. In just minutes, a message was encoded, transmitted, received, and decoded—perfectly and without any errors. The Navajo language, combined with a specially developed code, was unlike anything the Japanese had encountered. It was a perfect solution to the military's problem.

Soon after, the Marine Corps recruited 29 Navajo men to develop the code. These men, often referred to as the "First 29," were tasked with creating a code that could be used to communicate vital information quickly and accurately. They were not just creating a simple translation of English into Navajo. Instead, they developed a new system that used Navajo words to represent military terms, tactics, and equipment.

For example, the Navajo word for "turtle" was used to represent a tank, and the word for "chicken hawk" was used for a dive bomber. The code also incorporated a system to spell out words, using Navajo terms that corresponded with letters of the alphabet. This method allowed them to spell out place names or technical terms that didn't have a direct Navajo equivalent. The code was complex, but it was also flexible, fast, and, most importantly, impossible for the enemy to break.

After the code was developed, the Navajo Code Talkers were deployed to the Pacific Theater, where they participated in every major Marine operation in the Pacific from 1942 to 1945. They were at the forefront of some of the most intense battles of the war, including Guadalcanal, Tarawa, Saipan, Iwo Jima, and Okinawa. The Code Talkers were not only responsible for sending and receiving encoded messages but also for ensuring those messages were transmitted accurately and quickly, often under fire.

One of the most famous moments involving the Navajo Code Talkers occurred during the Battle of Iwo Jima. Over the course of the 36-day battle, six Navajo Code Talkers worked around the clock, transmitting more than 800 messages. Their work was critical in coordinating the Marine Corps' movements and ultimately in securing the island. Major Howard Connor, the signal officer of the 5th Marine Division, famously said, "Were it not for the Navajos, the Marines would never have taken Iwo Jima."

The success of the Navajo Code Talkers was not just due to the uniqueness of the Navajo language but also to the incredible bravery and dedication of these men. They operated in the most dangerous conditions, knowing that they were prime targets for the enemy. The Japanese knew that the Americans had some kind of new, unbreakable code, and they were desperate to capture a Code Talker to figure it out. But despite the danger, no Code Talker was ever captured, and the code remained unbroken throughout the war.

The Navajo Code Talkers were a vital part of the U.S. military's success in the Pacific. Their code allowed the Marines to communicate quickly and securely, giving them a significant advantage over the Japanese. But despite their crucial role, the Code Talkers' contributions were classified for many years after the war. They were sworn to secrecy, and it wasn't until 1968 that the program was declassified, and the Code Talkers could finally be recognized for their service.

The story of the Navajo Code Talkers is one of ingenuity, bravery, and patriotism. These men used their unique cultural heritage to create a code that saved countless lives and helped secure victory in one of the most critical theaters of World War II. Their story is a powerful reminder of how diverse backgrounds and unique skills can come together to achieve extraordinary things, even in the face of overwhelming odds.

For many years, the contributions of the Navajo Code Talkers were not widely known or appreciated. But today, their legacy is honored and celebrated, both within the Navajo Nation and across the United States. Monuments, films, books, and ceremonies have been dedicated to preserving their story and ensuring that future generations understand the vital role they played in the war.

In learning about the Navajo Code Talkers, we are reminded that heroism comes in many forms. Sometimes, it's found not in the roar of battle but in the quiet, determined work of those who use their unique skills to protect others. The Navajo Code Talkers were true American heroes, and their story continues to inspire people of all ages, reminding us of the power of language, culture, and courage in the fight for freedom.

African Soldiers in WWII: Fighting for a Cause

During World War II, the battlefields were filled with soldiers from around the globe, each fighting for their country, for freedom, and for a future free from tyranny. Among these brave warriors were African soldiers, men who traveled far from their homes to join the fight against the Axis powers. These soldiers came from various regions of Africa, including British and French colonies, and they played a crucial role in the Allied victory. Their stories are not only about courage and sacrifice but also about fighting for a cause greater than themselves, one that would resonate far beyond the battlefields of Europe and the deserts of North Africa.

As the war raged on, many African men found themselves drafted or volunteering to join the war effort. For some, it was a sense of duty to the colonial powers that ruled their homelands; for others, it was a chance to escape poverty or a desire to prove their worth on the global stage. Whatever their reasons, these men left behind their families, their communities, and the familiar landscapes of Africa to face an uncertain future in lands far away.

The experiences of African soldiers in World War II were as diverse as the men themselves. They served in various capacities, from infantrymen on the front lines to drivers, cooks, and laborers who kept the military machine running. Many were assigned to the British and French armies, where they fought alongside soldiers from all corners of the globe. In the British army, African soldiers were often grouped into units known as the King's African Rifles, a regiment that saw action in some of the war's most challenging theaters, including Burma, Madagascar, and Ethiopia.

In the North African campaign, African soldiers played a vital role in the fight against German and Italian forces. The deserts of North Africa were harsh and unforgiving, with scorching heat by day and freezing cold by night. The terrain was treacherous, with vast stretches of barren land that provided little cover from the enemy. Yet, despite these challenges, African soldiers demonstrated remarkable resilience and determination. They fought bravely in battles such as El Alamein, where their efforts helped turn the tide in favor of the Allies. Their knowledge of the land, ability to endure harsh conditions, and willingness to fight made them invaluable to the Allied forces.

Beyond the physical hardships of war, African soldiers also faced significant challenges related to race and colonialism. In many cases, they were treated as second-class soldiers, receiving lower pay and fewer benefits than their European counterparts. They often faced discrimination, not only from the enemy but also from within the ranks of the Allied forces. Despite these injustices, African soldiers remained committed to the cause. They fought with the hope that their contributions would be recognized and that their service would pave the way for greater rights and freedoms in their homelands.

For some African soldiers, the war offered a chance to challenge the colonial status quo. They saw the fight against fascism as part of a broader struggle for justice and equality. Leaders like Léopold Sédar Senghor, who would later become the first president of Senegal, served in the French army during the war. Senghor and others like him were inspired by the ideals of liberty and self-determination that the Allies claimed to be fighting for. They hoped that their service in the war would strengthen their demands for independence and better treatment for African people.

The bravery of African soldiers did not go unnoticed. In many instances, they earned the respect and admiration of their comrades and commanders. Stories of their heroism spread, such as the tale of the Nigerian soldier who single-handedly captured an enemy machine-gun post, or the Ghanaian trooper who rescued his wounded comrades under heavy fire. These acts of valor highlighted the courage and capability of African soldiers, challenging the racist stereotypes that had long been used to justify their subjugation.

As the war came to an end, African soldiers returned home to a world that was changing rapidly. The war had exposed the contradictions of colonialism, with African men fighting and dying for freedoms that they themselves did not fully enjoy. Many soldiers returned with a new sense of purpose, determined to fight for their rights and the rights of their people. Their experiences in the war fueled the growing movements for independence across Africa. The service of African soldiers in World War II became a symbol of the broader struggle for decolonization, and their stories inspired a new generation of leaders and activists.

The contributions of African soldiers in World War II were immense, yet for many years, their stories were largely overlooked or forgotten. It is only in recent years that historians and writers have begun to uncover and celebrate the role these men played in one of the most significant conflicts in human history. Their stories are a testament to the power of courage and conviction, and they remind us that the fight for freedom and justice is a global one.

For the young readers of today, the stories of African soldiers in World War II offer valuable lessons. These men showed that bravery knows no boundaries and that the fight for a just cause is worth the sacrifices it demands. They remind us that history is made not only by the famous figures whose names are etched in textbooks but also by the countless individuals who, in their own way, helped shape the world we live in. By learning about these remarkable soldiers, we honor their legacy and ensure that their contributions are never forgotten.

Chapter Ten

Women at War

The Night Witches: Soviet Female Pilots Who Terrified the Enemy

During World War II, the skies above Europe were often filled with the roar of engines and the crack of gunfire. But in the dead of night, a different kind of terror descended upon the German forces—one they never anticipated. This terror came not from a fearsome aircraft, but from a group of brave young women known as the Night Witches. These Soviet female pilots, officially called the 588th Night Bomber Regiment, struck fear into the hearts of the enemy, becoming one of the most remarkable and inspiring stories of World War II.

The Night Witches were not just any pilots. They were a group of women who defied the expectations of their time, stepping into roles traditionally reserved for men. In the Soviet Union during the early 1940s, women were encouraged to support the war effort in various ways, but few imagined that they would take to the skies as combat pilots. However, Marina Raskova, a famous Soviet aviator and the first female navigator in the Soviet Air Force, believed otherwise. With her determination, she persuaded the Soviet military to create an all-female aviation regiment.

The 588th Night Bomber Regiment was formed in 1942, and its members were mostly young women in their late teens and early twenties.

Many of them had little to no experience flying before the war, but they were eager to serve their country. These women trained rigorously, learning to fly under the most challenging conditions. They had to master the art of night flying, as their missions would be carried out under the cover of darkness to increase their chances of evading the enemy.

The aircraft they flew were far from the cutting-edge technology of the time. The Night Witches piloted the Polikarpov Po-2, a small, outdated biplane made primarily of wood and canvas. Originally designed as a training aircraft, the Po-2 was slow, with a top speed lower than that of many enemy planes. It had no armor to protect its pilots and could carry only two bombs at a time. But what the Po-2 lacked in power, it made up for in maneuverability. Its slow speed allowed it to fly low and close to the ground, making it difficult for enemy fighters to target.

The Night Witches turned their limitations into strengths. They developed tactics that exploited the unique characteristics of the Po-2. One of their most effective strategies was to cut their engines as they approached their targets. The silence of the gliding aircraft would catch the German forces off guard, earning the pilots their nickname. The only sound the enemy heard was the eerie whooshing of the wind as the biplanes swooped down to release their bombs. This tactic was so successful that it left the Germans in a constant state of fear, never knowing when the Night Witches might strike.

The Night Witches flew in pairs, with one plane drawing the attention of enemy searchlights and anti-aircraft fire while the other swooped in to drop its bombs. They carried out their missions with incredible bravery, flying multiple sorties each night. The regiment became so effective that it was said that any German pilot who downed one of the Night Witches would be automatically awarded the prestigious Iron Cross medal.

However, the life of a Night Witch was far from glamorous. The conditions they endured were harsh. The open cockpits of their planes exposed them to the freezing temperatures of the high-altitude night flights. They had no parachutes, as the planes were too small to accommodate them, and if they were shot down, they had little hope of survival. Despite these dangers, the women of the 588th Night Bomber Regiment showed unwavering courage. They flew over 30,000 missions during the war, dropping more than 23,000 tons of bombs on enemy targets.

One of the most notable members of the Night Witches was Nadezhda Popova, who became a legend for her daring exploits. She flew over 850 missions, surviving multiple crashes and being shot down several times. Popova's bravery and skill made her one of the most decorated pilots in the regiment, earning her the title of Hero of the Soviet Union, one of the highest honors in the country.

The Night Witches were not just exceptional pilots; they were also trailblazers for women in the military. At a time when many believed that women were not suited for combat roles, these young aviators proved that they could perform as well, if not better, than their male counterparts. Their success helped to challenge the traditional gender roles of the time, showing that women were capable of contributing to the war effort in ways that had never been imagined before.

The legacy of the Night Witches continues to inspire to this day. Their story is one of resilience, bravery, and determination in the face of overwhelming odds. They not only played a crucial role in the Soviet war effort but also left an indelible mark on history. The fear they instilled in their enemies and the respect they earned from their comrades are testaments to their extraordinary courage.

For young readers, the story of the Night Witches serves as a powerful reminder that bravery knows no gender. These women were ordinary individuals who, when faced with the extraordinary challenges of war, rose to the occasion and became heroes. They remind us that anyone, regardless of their background or circumstances, can make a difference in the world. The Night Witches didn't just fly planes—they soared above the limitations imposed on them, leaving a legacy that continues to inspire generations.

In the grand narrative of World War II, the Night Witches stand out not just for their tactical successes, but for their spirit and determination. Their story is one of those rare instances where reality exceeds the wildest imagination, making it one of the most action-packed and inspiring tales to emerge from the war. And as the night skies of history remember their bravery, so too do we pass on their legacy to inspire future generations.

Rosie the Riveter: The Women Who Built America's War Machines

During World War II, America faced one of its greatest challenges: a global conflict that required an unprecedented level of national unity and sacrifice. As the men went off to fight in the war, a new and essential force emerged on the home front—women. One of the most iconic symbols of this era is Rosie the Riveter, representing the countless women who stepped up to fill roles traditionally held by men, contributing to the war effort in ways that would change the course of history.

In the early 1940s, the United States found itself deeply entrenched in World War II. Factories that had once produced consumer goods quickly shifted to manufacturing tanks, planes, ships, and other vital military equipment. With millions of men enlisted in the military, the nation faced a significant labor shortage. To meet the demands of the war effort, the government and industry leaders began a nationwide campaign to recruit women into the workforce. This was a radical shift, as women had long been relegated to domestic roles or low-paying jobs. However, the need for workers was dire, and women were called upon to take on jobs that required strength, skill, and determination.

Rosie the Riveter became the face of this movement. She was not a real person, but rather a cultural icon, created to inspire and encourage women to join the workforce. The image of Rosie, with her rolled-up sleeves, flexed arm, and determined expression, was featured on posters, magazines, and advertisements across the country. The slogan "We Can Do It!" became a rallying cry for women everywhere, symbolizing their strength and capability.

Women from all walks of life answered the call. Housewives, teachers, nurses, and young women just out of school left their homes and classrooms to take up jobs in factories, shipyards, and other industries crucial to the war effort. These women, known as "Rosies," took on roles as riveters, welders, electricians, and machinists. They built airplanes, ships, and tanks, working long hours in challenging conditions to ensure that American troops had the equipment they needed to fight.

The work was demanding and often dangerous. Many of the women had never worked outside the home before, let alone in heavy industry. They had to learn new skills quickly, often with little training. The jobs required physical strength, precision, and attention to detail. Despite these challenges, the Rosies proved themselves more than capable. They worked side by side with men, earning their respect and admiration. Their contributions were essential to the success of the war effort, as they produced the weapons and machinery that helped secure victory.

The impact of Rosie the Riveter extended beyond the factories. The presence of women in the workforce challenged traditional gender roles and perceptions of what women could achieve. Before the war, women were expected to focus on homemaking and child-rearing, while men were the breadwinners. The war changed that dynamic, as women became the primary earners in many households. They gained financial independence, new skills, and a sense of pride in their work. This shift laid the groundwork for future movements for women's rights and equality.

The legacy of Rosie the Riveter is profound. The women who worked in the factories during World War II not only helped to win the war, but they also paved the way for future generations of women to pursue careers in fields previously dominated by men. They proved that women could excel in any job, regardless of societal expectations.

After the war ended, many of the Rosies were expected to return to their traditional roles at home. Some did, but many others continued to work, inspired by the independence and fulfillment they had found during the war years. The experience of working in the factories had changed them, and they were not content to return to the way things were before. This determination helped to fuel the women's rights movement in the years that followed, leading to greater opportunities and equality for women in the workforce.

The story of Rosie the Riveter is a testament to the power of determination, resilience, and teamwork. It is a reminder that in times of crisis, ordinary people can achieve extraordinary things when they come together for a common cause. The Rosies showed the world that women are capable of much more than society had previously allowed, and their contributions continue to inspire people today.

For young readers, the story of Rosic the Riveter offers important lessons about courage, perseverance, and the importance of standing up for what is right. It teaches that challenges can be overcome with hard work and determination and that everyone, regardless of gender, has something valuable to contribute. Rosie the Riveter's legacy lives on, not just as a symbol of the women who built America's war machines, but as a beacon of hope and inspiration for future generations.

Today, Rosie the Riveter is celebrated as an American icon, representing the strength and resilience of women during one of the most challenging times in history. Her story reminds us of the vital role women played in securing victory during World War II and the lasting impact they had on American society. The image of Rosie, with her confident pose and empowering message, continues to inspire people of all ages to believe in their own strength and ability to make a difference in the world.

As we reflect on the contributions of Rosie the Riveter and the women of World War II, we are reminded that history is not just shaped by generals and politicians, but by ordinary individuals who rise to the occasion when needed. The Rosies were mothers, daughters, sisters, and friends who answered the call to serve their country in its time of need. Their story is a powerful example of how collective effort and determination can overcome even the greatest challenges.

In learning about Rosie the Riveter, we gain a deeper understanding of the sacrifices and contributions made by women during World War II. We also recognize the enduring impact of their work, which helped to shape the modern world and advance the cause of equality. Rosie the Riveter's story is not just a tale from the past; it is a living legacy that continues to inspire and empower people today.

Chapter Eleven

The Power of Unity

The Christmas Truce: When Enemies Became Friends

On a cold December night in 1914, during the first Christmas of World War I, something extraordinary happened that would forever be remembered as a beacon of humanity amid the horrors of war. The Christmas Truce, as it came to be known, was a moment when the guns fell silent, and enemies became friends, if only for a short time. This remarkable event took place along the Western Front, where German and British soldiers, entrenched in muddy ditches, faced each other across a desolate No Man's Land.

The war had been raging for several months by this time, and the soldiers on both sides were weary, cold, and longing for the warmth and comfort of home. Christmas was a time traditionally spent with family, exchanging gifts, singing carols, and enjoying festive meals. But here they were, far from home, fighting in a war that seemed to have no end. Despite the bitterness and fear that pervaded the trenches, the spirit of Christmas began to seep through the cracks of conflict.

As Christmas Eve approached, an unusual stillness settled over the battlefield. The relentless gunfire and shelling that had become a daily occurrence suddenly ceased. The soldiers on both sides were puzzled by the quiet, but they were also relieved. For the first time in weeks, they could hear themselves think. They could feel the cold air on their faces without the accompanying terror of battle.

Then, something even more unexpected happened. From the German trenches, the sound of singing began to drift across No Man's Land. It was a familiar tune, one that the British soldiers recognized instantly: "Stille Nacht," known to them as "Silent Night." The voices were strong, clear, and filled with emotion. The British soldiers listened in amazement as their enemies sang a song that spoke of peace, love, and hope. Without thinking, they began to sing along in English. The two versions of the carol intertwined, creating a harmonious blend of voices that echoed across the battlefield.

The singing was the first step in breaking down the barriers that had separated these men for so long. Encouraged by the shared experience, a few brave souls from both sides began to climb out of their trenches. They cautiously made their way into No Man's Land, hands raised to show they were unarmed. At first, there was a palpable tension in the air. But as the soldiers approached each other, something miraculous happened. They smiled, they shook hands, and soon, they were exchanging gifts.

The gifts were simple, yet meaningful. Soldiers swapped chocolate, cigarettes, and even buttons from their uniforms. These small tokens of goodwill were given not out of obligation, but from a genuine desire to connect with the person on the other side. They spoke different languages, but they found ways to communicate through gestures and shared experiences. Some played soccer, using improvised balls made from whatever they could find. For a few precious hours, the battlefield was transformed into a place of laughter, camaraderie, and peace.

The Christmas Truce was not an official ceasefire; it was a spontaneous act of goodwill that spread like wildfire along the Western Front. News of the truce quickly reached other parts of the line, and soon, soldiers up and down the trenches were joining in. Officers who might have been expected to put a stop to such fraternization often turned a blind eye, recognizing the deep human need for connection, especially during the holiday season.

As the night wore on, the soldiers continued to talk, laugh, and share stories. They discovered that, despite the different uniforms and languages, they had much in common. They were all sons, brothers, and fathers. They all missed their families and yearned for the comfort of home. For that brief time, they were not enemies; they were simply men who wanted the same things: peace, warmth, and the chance to live their lives free from the fear of death.

But as dawn broke on Christmas Day, the reality of war began to creep back in. Orders came down from high command on both sides, reminding the soldiers of their duty. The truce, though beautiful, was not to last. Slowly, the men returned to their trenches, knowing that the fighting would soon resume. The brief moments of friendship and peace they had shared were like a dream, one that would be hard to hold onto once the war resumed.

The Christmas Truce of 1914 did not end the war, nor did it lead to a lasting peace. The conflict would continue for several more years, claiming the lives of millions. But the truce left a lasting impression on all who experienced it. It was a reminder that even in the darkest of times, the light of humanity can still shine through. The soldiers who participated in the truce never forgot the moment when they laid down their arms and reached out to the men they had been ordered to kill. It was a powerful testament to the fact that, at our core, we are all human, capable of kindness, compassion, and understanding, even in the most trying circumstances.

For the children reading this story today, the Christmas Truce is a lesson in the importance of empathy and the power of human connection. It shows that even in the midst of war, there is always room for understanding, for reaching out to others, and for finding common ground. It's a reminder that peace is not just the absence of conflict, but the presence of goodwill, friendship, and a shared desire for a better world.

As you think about the soldiers who participated in the Christmas Truce, remember that they were ordinary people, just like you. They faced extraordinary challenges, but they never lost sight of what truly mattered: love, friendship, and the hope for a brighter future. Their story is a beacon of hope, showing us that even in the most difficult times, we have the power to choose peace, to reach out to others, and to make the world a better place, one small act of kindness at a time.

The United Nations: Building a Peaceful Future

In the aftermath of World War II, the world was left reeling from the devastation and horror of a conflict that had engulfed nearly every corner of the globe. The war had claimed millions of lives, shattered cities, and left deep scars on the hearts and minds of those who had lived through it. As the dust settled, the world's leaders recognized the need for a new approach to international relations—one that could prevent such a catastrophe from ever happening again. It was out of this desire for lasting peace that the United Nations (UN) was born.

The United Nations was established in 1945, just months after the end of World War II, with a mission to promote peace, security, and cooperation among the nations of the world. Its founding was a direct response to the failures of the League of Nations, an earlier organization created after World War I that had been unable to prevent the outbreak of the second, even more devastating, global conflict. The leaders who formed the United Nations were determined not to repeat the mistakes of the past. They envisioned a world where countries could resolve their differences through dialogue and diplomacy rather than resorting to war.

The creation of the United Nations was nothing short of a monumental achievement. It brought together representatives from 50 countries, who gathered in San Francisco in April 1945 to draft the United Nations Charter. This charter would serve as the foundational document of the organization, outlining its goals, principles, and structure. The representatives spent months negotiating, debating, and crafting a document that would reflect the aspirations of a world hungry for peace. On October 24, 1945, the United Nations officially came into existence, and this date is now celebrated annually as United Nations Day.

One of the key goals of the United Nations was to prevent future conflicts by addressing the root causes of war. This included promoting social and economic development, protecting human rights, and fostering cooperation between nations. The UN was designed to be a forum where countries could come together to discuss their differences, negotiate solutions, and work collaboratively on global challenges. It was an ambitious vision, but one that was rooted in the belief that peace was not only possible but essential for the survival of humanity.

At the heart of the United Nations is the General Assembly, where all member states have an equal voice. Here, representatives from every country can discuss and vote on a wide range of issues, from international security to environmental protection. The General Assembly is a unique institution in that it gives every country, regardless of its size or power, an opportunity to be heard. This reflects the UN's commitment to inclusivity and the belief that peace can only be achieved when all voices are considered.

In addition to the General Assembly, the United Nations also established the Security Council, which is responsible for maintaining international peace and security. The Security Council has the authority to make binding decisions that member states are obligated to follow. It can impose sanctions, authorize the use of force, and deploy peacekeeping missions to conflict zones around the world. The Security Council's work is often challenging, as its decisions must be supported by the five permanent members—China, France, Russia, the United Kingdom, and the United States—all of whom have the power to veto any resolution. Despite these challenges, the Security Council has played a critical role in preventing conflicts and restoring peace in many parts of the world.

One of the most significant achievements of the United Nations has been its role in peacekeeping. Since its inception, the UN has deployed peacekeeping missions to dozens of conflict zones, where blue-helmeted soldiers and civilian personnel work to maintain ceasefires, protect civilians, and support the implementation of peace agreements. These missions are often dangerous and complex, but they have helped to stabilize regions that might otherwise have descended into chaos. The presence of UN peacekeepers has given hope to millions of people living in conflict-affected areas and has demonstrated the organization's commitment to building a peaceful future.

Beyond its efforts to prevent and resolve conflicts, the United Nations has also been instrumental in promoting human rights. The adoption of the Universal Declaration of Human Rights in 1948 was a landmark moment in the history of the UN and the world. This document, which was drafted by representatives from different cultural and legal backgrounds, sets out the fundamental rights and freedoms to which every person is entitled. It has since become the foundation for international human rights law and has inspired countless individuals and movements to fight for justice and equality.

The United Nations has also worked tirelessly to address global challenges that could threaten peace and security. From poverty and hunger to climate change and pandemics, the UN has launched numerous initiatives aimed at improving the lives of people around the world. These efforts are rooted in the understanding that peace is not just the absence of war but the presence of conditions that allow all people to live with dignity and opportunity. The UN's Sustainable Development Goals, adopted in 2015, represent a global blueprint for achieving these conditions by 2030.

As we reflect on the history of the United Nations, it is clear that the organization has made remarkable strides in its mission to build a peaceful future. While challenges remain, the UN's work has saved countless lives, prevented conflicts, and brought countries together in ways that were once unimaginable. The United Nations continues to be a beacon of hope for a world that is still grappling with the legacy of war and the pursuit of peace.

For young readers, the story of the United Nations is a powerful reminder that even in the face of immense challenges, it is possible to create positive change. The UN's founders were driven by a belief in the potential for humanity to overcome its darkest moments and to build a future where peace, justice, and cooperation prevail. It is a story that inspires us to look beyond our differences and to work together to create a world where everyone can thrive. As we look to the future, the United Nations remains a vital institution in the quest for a more peaceful and just world, and its story is one that will continue to inspire generations to come.

Chapter Twelve

The Holocaust: Stories of Survival

The Courage of the Survivors

World War II was a time of immense turmoil and suffering, but it was also a period that revealed the strength of the human spirit in ways that continue to inspire us today. Among the countless stories of bravery and resilience, the courage of the survivors stands out as a beacon of hope and determination. These individuals, many of whom were just children at the time, faced unimaginable horrors. Yet, they emerged with stories that not only recount their struggles but also highlight the power of hope, endurance, and the will to survive against all odds.

Imagine waking up one day to find your world turned upside down. Everything that was once familiar and safe is now dangerous and uncertain. This was the reality for millions of people during World War II, particularly those targeted by the Nazi regime. Families were torn apart, homes were destroyed, and communities were devastated. For many, the fight for survival became a daily battle, not just against the physical dangers of war, but against the crushing weight of fear and despair.

One of the most harrowing aspects of this time was the Holocaust, during which six million Jews were systematically persecuted and murdered by the Nazis. Among those who survived, there are stories that reveal incredible acts of bravery and resilience. Take the story of

Anne Frank, for example. Anne was just a young girl when her family was forced into hiding to escape the Nazis. For two years, she lived in a cramped secret annex with her family and others, always under the threat of being discovered. Despite the fear and uncertainty, Anne kept a diary in which she expressed her hopes, dreams, and observations about the world around her. Her words, written during such a dark time, continue to resonate with readers around the world, reminding us of the importance of hope even in the bleakest of circumstances.

Another remarkable story is that of Elie Wiesel, a young boy who was taken to Auschwitz, one of the most infamous concentration camps, with his family. The conditions in the camp were beyond horrific—cruelty, starvation, and death were everyday occurrences. Yet, Elie survived. He later wrote about his experiences in his book *Night*, which has become one of the most powerful testimonies of the Holocaust. In his writing, Elie shares not just the physical pain of his experiences, but the deep emotional and spiritual struggles he faced. His story is one of survival not just of the body, but of the spirit, as he grappled with the loss of his family, his faith, and his innocence.

In addition to the Jews, other groups were also targeted by the Nazis, including Romani people, disabled individuals, political dissidents, and more. The courage of survivors from these groups is equally inspiring. For instance, the story of Zlata Filipovic, a young girl from

Sarajevo, shows how the resilience of the human spirit can shine even in the darkest times. Although Zlata's story is from a later conflict, it mirrors the experiences of many children during WWII. Zlata kept a diary during the Siege of Sarajevo, documenting the daily struggles of living in a war zone. Her diary, like Anne Frank's, became a symbol of the innocence lost during times of conflict and the strength required to keep going.

Survivors of World War II did not just endure physical hardship; they also had to cope with the psychological and emotional scars left by their experiences. Many were haunted by nightmares and memories of the atrocities they witnessed. Yet, their courage lay in their ability to rebuild their lives, to find meaning and purpose despite their pasts. For some, this meant sharing their stories with the world, ensuring that future generations would never forget the horrors of war. For others, it meant quietly carrying on, building families and communities, and finding ways to contribute to the world despite the pain they had endured.

One of the most poignant aspects of these survivors' stories is the way they highlight the importance of community and solidarity. During the war, countless individuals risked their lives to help others, whether by hiding them from the Nazis, providing food and shelter, or simply offering a kind word or gesture. These acts of kindness, no matter how small, provided a lifeline for those struggling to survive. They also demonstrate the incredible impact that compassion and empathy can have, even in the most difficult circumstances.

As we reflect on the courage of the survivors, it is important to remember that their stories are not just about the past; they carry lessons for the present and the future. Their resilience teaches us the importance of standing up against injustice, of helping those in need, and of never losing hope, even when the odds seem insurmountable. These stories also remind us that, even in the darkest times, there is always light to be found—whether in the kindness of a stranger, the love of family, or the simple act of surviving another day.

For young readers, the stories of these survivors offer a powerful message: that courage is not the absence of fear, but the ability to face fear and continue on. It is the strength to hold onto hope when everything else seems lost, and the determination to make the world a better place, even in the face of overwhelming adversity. As we honor the memories of those who lived through World War II, let us carry forward the lessons of their courage, using them to inspire our own lives and the lives of future generations.

The courage of the survivors of World War II is a testament to the resilience of the human spirit. Their stories, filled with pain, loss, and hardship, are also stories of hope, strength, and endurance. They remind us that, even in the face of unimaginable horror, it is possible to survive, to rebuild, and to find meaning and purpose in life. Their bravery continues to inspire us, teaching us that no matter how dark the world may seem, there is always the possibility of light and the promise of a better tomorrow.

The Importance of Remembering

World War II, one of the most significant events in human history, profoundly shaped the world as we know it today. The stories of bravery, sacrifice, and resilience that emerged from this period are not just tales of the past; they are lessons that continue to resonate with us. As we journey through the stories of remarkable figures from WWII, we come to understand why it is so crucial to remember this pivotal time in history. For young readers, the importance of remembering World War II is not just about knowing what happened but understanding why it matters today and for the future.

The events of World War II were set in motion by a complex web of political, economic, and social factors that led to one of the deadliest conflicts in history. As nations clashed, entire societies were drawn into a war that spanned the globe. The war brought out the worst in humanity—destruction, hatred, and unimaginable suffering. But it also revealed extraordinary acts of heroism, kindness, and unity. These stories, often passed down through generations, serve as a reminder of both the horrors of war and the strength of the human spirit.

One of the primary reasons we must remember World War II is to honor the memory of those who fought, suffered, and died during this time.

Millions of soldiers, civilians, and resistance fighters from all corners of the world gave their lives in the struggle against tyranny and oppression. Their sacrifices ensured the freedoms we enjoy today, and by remembering them, we ensure that their efforts were not in vain. The stories of these brave individuals inspire us to value peace and to stand up against injustice whenever it arises.

For children growing up in a world that often seems distant from the events of World War II, it can be challenging to grasp the full impact of the war. However, by learning about the remarkable figures who lived through it, young readers can connect with history on a personal level. These stories show that the war was not just about battles and military strategy; it was about real people—ordinary men, women, and even children—who faced extraordinary circumstances. They remind us that courage, kindness, and resilience are values that transcend time and that we, too, can make a difference in our own lives.

Moreover, remembering World War II is essential in ensuring that the mistakes of the past are not repeated. The war was born out of extreme ideologies, intolerance, and a failure of diplomacy. By studying this period, we learn about the dangers of unchecked power, the consequences of prejudice, and the importance of standing up for what is right. These lessons are particularly important for young readers, who will grow up to become the leaders and decision-makers of tomorrow. Understanding the causes and consequences of World War II helps to build a foundation for a more just and peaceful world.

The stories of World War II also teach us about the power of unity and cooperation. The war brought together people from different countries, cultures, and backgrounds to fight for a common cause. It showed that when people work together, they can overcome even the most daunting challenges. This message of unity is especially important in today's world, where divisions and conflicts still exist. By remembering the cooperation that helped bring an end to World War II, we are reminded of the strength that comes from working together.

In addition to honoring the past and learning from it, remembering World War II is also about preserving the memory of those who lived through it. As the years pass, fewer and fewer people who experienced the war firsthand are still with us. It is up to the younger generations to keep their stories alive. By reading about and reflecting on the experiences of those who lived during World War II, we help to ensure that their memories are not lost to time. This is not just a matter of historical record; it is about keeping alive the human stories that give meaning to history.

For children, learning about World War II can be a way to develop empathy and understanding. The stories of those who suffered and survived the war teach us about the importance of compassion and the need to help others in times of need. They show that even in the darkest of times, there is always hope, and that even the smallest acts of kindness can have a significant impact. By remembering the war, we are reminded of our shared humanity and our responsibility to care for one another.

In remembering World War II, we also recognize the importance of peace. The war was a stark reminder of the devastating consequences of conflict. The stories of destruction and loss that emerged from the war serve as a powerful reminder of why peace is so precious. For young readers, understanding the value of peace is crucial. It teaches them to appreciate the world they live in and to work towards a future where such a conflict never happens again.

Finally, remembering World War II helps us to appreciate the progress that has been made since the war ended. The world has come a long way in terms of human rights, democracy, and international cooperation. However, the stories of World War II remind us that these achievements were hard-won and that they must be protected and nurtured. By looking back at the struggles and triumphs of the past, we are better equipped to face the challenges of the future.

In conclusion, the importance of remembering World War II cannot be overstated. For young readers, these stories are more than just historical accounts; they are lessons in courage, kindness, and the power of the human spirit. By remembering the remarkable figures of World War II, we honor their legacy, learn from their experiences, and commit to building a better world for future generations. The stories of World War II are not just tales of the past—they are a guide for the future, showing us the importance of standing up for what is right, working together, and never forgetting the lessons of history.

Chapter Thirteen

Stories of Rescue

Operation Pied Piper: Evacuating Children to Safety

During the dark days of World War II, as bombs fell from the skies and armies clashed across Europe, an extraordinary operation was undertaken to protect the most vulnerable—the children. This operation, known as Operation Pied Piper, was one of the largest and most complex evacuation efforts in history. It was a story of bravery, resilience, and the unwavering love of parents determined to keep their children safe amidst the horrors of war.

The year was 1939, and the specter of war loomed heavily over Britain. The government, aware of the devastating impact that air raids had during World War I, anticipated that major cities like London, Birmingham, and Liverpool would be prime targets for enemy bombers. The fear was palpable; the lives of thousands of children were at risk, and something had to be done to ensure their safety. Thus, the government devised a plan—Operation Pied Piper, named after the legend of the Pied Piper of Hamelin, who led the children of the town to safety.

On September 1, 1939, just two days before Britain officially declared war on Germany, the operation began. Over the course of just a few days, nearly 1.5 million people were evacuated, most of them children. These young evacuees were sent away from the industrial cities and into the relative safety of the countryside. But this was no simple journey. For many children, it was the first time they had ever left home, and the experience was filled with both fear and excitement.

Imagine being a child of just six or seven years old, clutching a small suitcase packed with your most treasured belongings. You're wearing a gas mask slung over your shoulder, a name tag pinned to your coat, and in your hand, a label with your destination. Your parents, who you have never been apart from, are waving goodbye, trying to hold back tears as they reassure you that everything will be fine. The sound of trains filled with evacuees echoed across the stations, and the sight of thousands of children, some smiling, others with tear-streaked faces, was both heartwarming and heart-wrenching.

The children didn't know where they were going, and many didn't understand why they had to leave. For the younger ones, it was an adventure—a chance to see the countryside, to live in a big house, perhaps even on a farm. But for the older children, the reality was much harder to bear. They knew that they were being sent away because their homes were not safe, that the threat of bombs was very real, and that there was no telling when, or if, they would see their parents again.

Upon arriving in the countryside, the children were met by volunteers who helped to place them in foster homes. Some were lucky enough to be welcomed into warm and loving households, where they were treated as part of the family. Others were not so fortunate. The sudden influx of evacuees put a strain on rural communities, and not all hosts were prepared or willing to take in the children. Some evacuees were placed in homes where they were treated as little more than unpaid labor, expected to work on farms or in the household.

Yet, despite these challenges, many children found ways to adapt. They formed new friendships, learned to live in environments vastly different from the city streets they were used to, and discovered a sense of independence. Schools were set up in village halls, and local teachers did their best to continue the children's education. For some, the countryside became a place of solace, a temporary escape from the grim realities of war.

However, Operation Pied Piper was not without its complications. The logistics of moving such a vast number of children were staggering. Trains were packed, and the government had to coordinate with schools, local authorities, and volunteer organizations to ensure the safety and well-being of the evacuees. There were instances of confusion and chaos, with children being sent to the wrong destinations or siblings being separated. Communication between parents and their evacuated children was difficult, and letters often took weeks to arrive.

The emotional toll on the evacuees and their families was immense. Parents, particularly mothers, were left behind in cities that would soon be under bombardment. They had to cope with the constant fear for their own safety while worrying about their children in distant, unfamiliar places. The children, too, struggled with homesickness, longing for the comfort of their families and the familiar sights and sounds of home. Some evacuees were so distressed that they were sent back to their parents, even though it meant returning to the dangers of the city.

Despite the hardships, the evacuation was a success in many ways. It is estimated that tens of thousands of lives were saved because these children were moved out of harm's way. Operation Pied Piper became a symbol of the collective effort to protect the innocent during a time of unimaginable peril. The bravery of the children, many of whom showed incredible resilience, and the dedication of those who took them in, is remembered as one of the most inspiring aspects of the war.

As the war dragged on, some children were evacuated multiple times, depending on where the fighting was most intense. Others remained in the countryside for the duration of the conflict. When the war finally ended in 1945, the return home was often bittersweet. The children had grown up; some barely recognized the cities they had left behind, which were now scarred by years of bombing. Families were reunited, but the war had left its mark on everyone. The experiences of evacuation shaped an entire generation, leaving them with memories of both the kindness of strangers and the pain of separation.

Operation Pied Piper remains one of the most remarkable and heartwarming stories of World War II. It is a tale of ordinary people coming together to do something extraordinary—protecting the future by safeguarding the lives of children. The operation showed that even in the darkest times, there is light, as communities opened their homes and hearts to those in need. The children of Operation Pied Piper, with their courage and resilience, became a testament to the strength of the human spirit in the face of adversity.

The Hidden Village of Le Chambon: A Safe Haven for Refugees

In the heart of Nazi-occupied France, during the dark days of World War II, there was a small village that stood as a beacon of hope and humanity. The village of Le Chambon-sur-Lignon, nestled in the mountainous region of the Vivarais Plateau, became a symbol of resistance, not through weapons or battles, but through compassion, bravery, and unwavering moral conviction. The story of Le Chambon is one of the most remarkable tales of heroism during World War II, demonstrating that even in the face of great danger, ordinary people can do extraordinary things.

The villagers of Le Chambon were mostly Huguenots, a Protestant minority in France with a long history of persecution. Perhaps it was this shared history of suffering that made them especially sensitive to the plight of others. When World War II erupted and the Nazi regime began its campaign of terror against Jews, the people of Le Chambon, led by their pastor André Trocmé and his wife Magda, made a collective decision to offer sanctuary to those in need.

The decision to help was not an easy one. The risks were immense. Nazi soldiers frequently patrolled the region, and anyone caught aiding Jews faced immediate arrest, deportation, or even execution. But the people of Le Chambon were guided by a deep sense of morality and a strong belief in doing what was right, no matter the cost. Pastor Trocmé often reminded his congregation of their duty to resist evil, famously declaring that they should "do the will of God, not of men."

As the Nazi persecution intensified, Jewish families, including many children, began to arrive in Le Chambon. The villagers opened their homes, schools, and farms to these refugees, offering them food, shelter, and protection. They did so without hesitation, treating their new guests as members of their own community. It wasn't just a few courageous individuals who participated; nearly every family in the village took part in the effort. This collective resistance was a powerful statement against the horrors of the Holocaust.

One of the most remarkable aspects of Le Chambon's story is how the villagers managed to keep their activities hidden from the authorities for so long. They developed an intricate network of communication and support. When word came that Nazi patrols were approaching, villagers would quickly hide their Jewish guests in barns, cellars, or in the dense forests that surrounded the village. Children were taught to keep quiet about the strangers in their homes, and everyone in the village understood the importance of secrecy.

The people of Le Chambon also went to great lengths to create false identity papers for the refugees, allowing them to pass as non-Jews and avoid arrest. These documents were crafted with incredible precision and care, often involving the collaboration of local officials who were sympathetic to the cause. In some cases, entire Jewish families were able to travel to neutral countries like Switzerland, where they would be safe from Nazi persecution, thanks to these forged papers.

Life in Le Chambon during this time was anything but ordinary. The constant threat of discovery hung over the village like a dark cloud. Yet, despite the danger, there was a strong sense of unity and purpose among the villagers. They knew that their actions were making a real difference in the lives of the refugees, and that knowledge gave them the strength to continue. The children of the village, too, played a crucial role. They befriended the Jewish children, helping them adjust to their new surroundings and offering them comfort in a time of great fear and uncertainty.

There were several close calls when the villagers' efforts nearly came to an end. On one occasion, the Gestapo—the Nazi secret police—arrived in Le Chambon, demanding that Pastor Trocmé hand over a list of all the Jews in the village. Trocmé refused, stating simply that he did not know the difference between Jews and non-Jews. His courage and calm defiance left the Gestapo agents stunned, and they left the village empty-handed. This was just one of many instances where the resolve of the villagers was tested, yet they never wavered in their commitment to protecting the innocent.

The impact of Le Chambon's actions during the war was profound. It is estimated that the village and its surrounding areas saved the lives of around 3,500 Jews, many of them children. This incredible feat was accomplished without any formal organization or outside support; it was simply the result of a community coming together to do what they believed was right.

After the war, the story of Le Chambon remained relatively unknown for many years. The villagers did not seek recognition or accolades for their actions; they had done what they believed any decent person would do. However, as the years passed and the full extent of the Holocaust became known, the world began to learn of the incredible bravery and compassion that had been shown in this small French village.

In 1981, Yad Vashem, the Holocaust remembrance center in Israel, honored Pastor André Trocmé, his wife Magda, and the entire village of Le Chambon-sur-Lignon with the title of "Righteous Among the Nations," a recognition given to non-Jews who risked their lives to save Jews during the Holocaust. This recognition brought the story of Le Chambon to a global audience, ensuring that the legacy of the villagers' actions would never be forgotten.

The story of Le Chambon is not just a tale of heroism during a time of war; it is a reminder of the power of community, compassion, and moral courage. It shows that even in the darkest times, there are those who will stand up for what is right, regardless of the risks. For the children who read this story, it is a powerful example of how ordinary people can make an extraordinary difference in the world. Le Chambon-sur-Lignon will forever be remembered as a safe haven, a place where the light of humanity shone brightly against the backdrop of one of history's darkest chapters.

Chapter Fourteen

Lessons from History

Learning from the Past: The Legacy of WWII

World War II was one of the most significant events in modern history, shaping the world in ways that continue to resonate today. For young readers, understanding the legacy of this global conflict is essential not just for learning about the past but also for gaining valuable lessons that can be applied to their lives. The stories of bravery, sacrifice, and resilience from World War II are more than just historical accounts; they are timeless lessons that can inspire children to understand the importance of courage, unity, and standing up for what is right.

As we delve into the legacy of World War II, it's important to recognize that the war was fought not just by soldiers on battlefields but by ordinary people who rose to extraordinary challenges. These individuals, many of whom were no older than the children reading this book, displayed remarkable courage and determination. They faced daunting circumstances, from bombings to invasions, yet they found ways to resist oppression and protect their communities. Their actions remind us that even in the darkest times, hope can shine through, and that each person has the power to make a difference.

One of the key lessons from World War II is the importance of standing up against injustice. The war began because of the unchecked aggression and expansion of Nazi Germany, fueled by ideologies of hatred and supremacy. The consequences of allowing such ideologies to spread unchecked were devastating, leading to the deaths of millions of innocent people. This tragic chapter in history teaches us that when we see wrongs being committed, we must speak out and take action. Whether it's standing up to a bully at school or speaking out against unfair treatment, the legacy of World War II encourages us to be courageous and to fight for justice and equality.

Another important aspect of the war's legacy is the power of unity. During World War II, people from different countries, cultures, and backgrounds came together to fight a common enemy. The Allied forces, which included the United States, the United Kingdom, the Soviet Union, and many others, were able to defeat the Axis powers because they worked together despite their differences. This unity extended beyond the battlefield. On the home front, families, communities, and nations pulled together, making sacrifices and supporting one another to contribute to the war effort. This collective strength teaches us that when we work together, we can overcome even the greatest challenges. In today's world, where differences often divide us, the legacy of World War II serves as a powerful reminder that unity is our greatest strength.

World War II also left us with lessons on the value of perseverance and resilience. The war brought about unimaginable hardships, from the devastation of cities to the loss of loved ones. Yet, in the face of these challenges, people found ways to carry on. Stories of children in London who continued their education in underground shelters during air raids, or of families who rebuilt their lives after their homes were destroyed, are testaments to the human spirit's ability to endure and overcome. These stories inspire us to keep going, even when things seem difficult, and to never lose hope, no matter how dire the situation.

The war also highlighted the importance of remembering and learning from history. After World War II, the world vowed to never let such a tragedy happen again. The United Nations was established to promote peace and cooperation among nations, and many countries adopted policies to prevent the rise of dictatorships and to protect human rights. These efforts reflect the understanding that history must be remembered to avoid repeating its mistakes. For young readers, this means that learning about World War II is not just about understanding what happened, but also about taking these lessons to heart. By remembering the sacrifices made and the horrors endured, we can all play a part in ensuring that such events are never repeated.

The legacy of World War II also includes the recognition of the power of kindness and compassion, even in the midst of war. There are countless stories of individuals who, at great personal risk, helped those in need. From the villagers of Le Chambon-sur-Lignon who hid

Jewish refugees, to the soldiers who shared their rations with starving civilians, these acts of kindness remind us that compassion can thrive even in the most challenging circumstances. These stories teach us that helping others, even when it's difficult, is a vital part of being human. They encourage us to look for ways to be kind and generous in our own lives, knowing that even small acts can have a big impact.

Finally, the legacy of World War II is a call to action for future generations. The freedoms and peace that many enjoy today were hard-won, and it is the responsibility of each new generation to protect and preserve them. This means being informed, staying engaged in the world around us, and being willing to stand up for what is right. The stories of World War II heroes inspire us to be brave, to work together, and to never forget the lessons of the past. They remind us that we all have the power to make a difference, and that by learning from history, we can help build a better, more peaceful future.

In conclusion, the legacy of World War II is rich with lessons that continue to be relevant today. It teaches us the importance of standing up against injustice, the power of unity, the value of perseverance, the necessity of remembering history, the impact of kindness, and the responsibility to protect the freedoms we enjoy. These lessons are not just for the history books; they are for all of us to learn, live by, and pass on to the next generation. As we reflect on the remarkable stories from this pivotal time, we are reminded that each of us has the potential to be a force for good in the world, just as those who came before us did during World War II.

How Today's Kids Can Make a Difference

During World War II, the world witnessed remarkable acts of courage, kindness, and resilience. The heroes of that time, many of whom were ordinary people, made extraordinary sacrifices to protect their countries, communities, and the principles of freedom and justice. While the events of WWII occurred decades ago, the lessons learned and the values upheld during that time remain relevant today. Even though today's kids may not be called upon to face the exact challenges of that era, they still have the power to make a significant difference in the world around them. By understanding the past, embracing the values demonstrated by the heroes of WWII, and applying these lessons to their own lives, young people can contribute to creating a better, more compassionate, and just world.

One of the most important lessons from WWII is the power of standing up for what is right, even when it is difficult or dangerous. The brave individuals who resisted oppression, protected the vulnerable, and fought against tyranny did so because they believed in the importance of justice and freedom. Today's kids can honor their legacy by standing up against bullying, discrimination, and injustice in their own communities. Whether it's defending a classmate who is being picked on, speaking out against unfair treatment, or supporting causes that promote equality and human rights, young people have the ability to be modern-day heroes. They can use their voices to make a difference, just as the heroes of WWII used theirs to stand up to oppression.

Another critical lesson from WWII is the importance of empathy and compassion. During the war, countless lives were saved by individuals who showed kindness and generosity to those in need, often at great personal risk. The stories of people like Irena Sendler, who smuggled Jewish children out of the Warsaw Ghetto, and Nicholas Winton, who organized the rescue of hundreds of children from Nazi-occupied Czechoslovakia, demonstrate the profound impact that compassion can have.

Today's kids can make a difference by practicing empathy in their everyday lives. This might involve helping a friend who is going through a tough time, volunteering at a local charity, or simply being kind and considerate to others. By putting themselves in someone else's shoes and acting with kindness, young people can contribute to a more compassionate and understanding world.

The heroes of WWII also teach us the value of resilience and perseverance in the face of adversity. Many of the individuals who played crucial roles in the war effort faced incredible hardships, yet they refused to give up. The soldiers who fought in the Battle of Britain, the women who took on traditionally male roles in factories, and the resistance fighters who risked their lives to sabotage enemy operations all demonstrated remarkable determination and grit. Today's kids can channel this same resilience when they encounter challenges in their own lives. Whether it's working hard to achieve their goals, staying positive during difficult times, or bouncing back from setbacks, young people can learn to persevere just as the heroes of WWII did. This resilience will not only help them overcome obstacles but also inspire others to do the same.

WWII also highlights the importance of working together for a common cause. The success of the Allied forces was due in large part to the collaboration between different nations, communities, and individuals. People from diverse backgrounds came together to fight for a shared goal: the defeat of tyranny and the restoration of peace. Today's kids can make a difference by recognizing the value of teamwork and collaboration in their own lives. Whether it's working with classmates on a school project, participating in community service, or joining a club or organization that promotes positive change, young people can achieve great things when they work together. By embracing teamwork and cooperation, they can contribute to solving the challenges of today, just as the Allied forces did during WWII.

One of the most enduring legacies of WWII is the importance of remembering the past and learning from it. The horrors of the Holocaust, the devastation of the war, and the sacrifices made by so many people serve as powerful reminders of what can happen when hatred and intolerance go unchecked. Today's kids can make a difference by educating themselves about history and reflecting on the lessons it teaches. By learning about the past, they can better understand the consequences of actions and decisions and work to ensure that such atrocities are never repeated. Additionally, young people can honor the memory of those who fought and died in WWII by participating in commemorative events, visiting museums, or reading books and watching documentaries about the war. This awareness and understanding of history can empower them to make informed decisions and take actions that promote peace and prevent future conflicts.

Finally, the stories of WWII heroes teach us that even small actions can have a big impact. Many of the people who made a difference during the war did so through seemingly small gestures of kindness, bravery, or resistance. Whether it was hiding a neighbor from the authorities, sharing food with a stranger, or spreading hope through a simple act of kindness, these small actions contributed to the larger effort to defeat evil and restore peace. Today's kids can make a difference by recognizing the power of small actions in their own lives. Whether it's picking up litter in their neighborhood, helping a younger sibling with homework, or writing a letter of support to someone in need, these small acts of kindness and responsibility can create a ripple effect of positive change. Just as the small acts of courage and kindness during WWII had a profound impact, so too can the actions of today's young people make a difference in the world around them.

In conclusion, the lessons of WWII are as relevant today as they were more than seventy years ago. By standing up for what is right, practicing empathy and compassion, demonstrating resilience, working together, learning from history, and recognizing the power of small actions, today's kids can make a significant difference in their communities and the world. The heroes of WWII showed us that ordinary people are capable of extraordinary things when they are guided by courage, kindness, and a sense of justice. By following in their footsteps, young people can become the heroes of their own time, contributing to a world that is more just, compassionate, and peaceful for all.

Chapter Fifteen

Heroes of the Home Front

Rationing and Resourcefulness: Life During Wartime

During World War II, life changed drastically for millions of people around the world, including children. As the war raged on, resources became scarce, and everyone had to adjust to a new way of living. This period of rationing and resourcefulness taught kids valuable lessons about courage, creativity, and the importance of working together. It was a time when even the smallest acts of saving and sharing could make a huge difference, and children played a vital role in the war effort.

As the war began, many countries introduced rationing systems to ensure that everyone had access to essential goods like food, clothing, and fuel. Rationing meant that families could only buy a certain amount of these items each week. Instead of going to the store and buying as much as they wanted, they had to use special ration books that limited their purchases. These ration books were filled with stamps, and each stamp allowed the holder to buy a specific amount of a particular item. For many children, these ration books became a symbol of the challenges and sacrifices that everyone was making for the war effort.

In Britain, for example, the government introduced rationing in 1940, shortly after the war began. This meant that everyone, from the youngest child to the oldest grandparent, had to adjust their eating habits. Foods like sugar, butter, and meat were in short supply, and families had to make do with what they had. This led to the rise of creative cooking, where mothers and even children learned to cook meals with limited ingredients. They made use of every scrap of food, turning leftovers into new dishes and finding clever ways to stretch their rations. A typical meal might consist of potatoes, vegetables, and a small portion of meat or fish, if they were lucky enough to have it. Desserts were often simple, using ingredients like carrots to sweeten cakes when sugar was unavailable.

For many kids, this was a time to learn the value of food and not to waste anything. They were encouraged to eat everything on their plates and not to ask for more than they needed. Schools played a big role in teaching children about rationing, with lessons on nutrition and the importance of sharing resources. Children were taught to appreciate the effort that went into growing and preparing food, and they learned how to make the most of what they had. This education helped foster a sense of responsibility and teamwork among young people, who understood that their actions could directly support the war effort.

In addition to food, clothing was also rationed during the war. This meant that families couldn't just go out and buy new clothes whenever they wanted. Instead, they had to make do with what they had, often repairing or altering old clothes to make them last longer. Mothers became experts at patching up holes and sewing on buttons, while children learned how to knit and mend their own clothes. This period of resourcefulness led to the popular saying, "Make do and mend," which became a mantra for many households.

Children also got creative with their toys and games during the war. With materials like metal and rubber needed for the war effort, there were fewer new toys available. Instead of buying toys, kids often made their own from whatever materials they could find. A tin can could become a toy car, and old rags could be sewn together to make a doll. These homemade toys were often treasured because they were made with love and imagination. This spirit of creativity and resourcefulness was a silver lining in the midst of the hardships, as kids learned to find joy in the simplest things.

The war also brought about the "Dig for Victory" campaign, which encouraged families to grow their own food in gardens and allotments. Even children got involved, planting vegetables and learning how to care for their gardens. This not only helped provide extra food for the family but also taught kids valuable lessons about hard work and patience. Growing food from seed to harvest was a rewarding experience, and it gave children a sense of pride in contributing to their family's well-being.

Beyond their homes, children were also involved in collecting materials for the war effort. Scrap metal, rubber, and paper were all needed to produce weapons, vehicles, and other supplies. Kids would go door-to-door collecting these items, often organizing scrap drives with their friends. These collections were more than just a way to pass the time; they were a crucial part of supporting the soldiers on the front lines. Every piece of metal or rubber collected could be turned into something that would help win the war, and children were proud to play their part.

Despite the challenges of rationing, there was a strong sense of community and shared purpose during the war. Neighbors looked out for one another, sharing food and resources when needed. Children learned to be resilient and to find happiness in the little things, like a rare treat of sweets or a new toy made from scraps. The hardships of the war brought families closer together, as they supported each other through difficult times.

For many children, the war years were a time of learning and growing. They developed skills that would stay with them for the rest of their lives, such as cooking, sewing, and gardening. They also learned the importance of helping others and being resourceful in the face of adversity. These lessons of rationing and resourcefulness shaped a generation of young people who understood the value of hard work, sacrifice, and community.

In the end, the wartime experiences of rationing and resourcefulness weren't just about getting by with less; they were about making the most of what you had and finding strength in the face of hardship. The children who lived through this time emerged with a deep appreciation for the simple things in life and a determination to make the world a better place. Their stories remind us that even in the darkest times, there is light to be found in the courage, creativity, and kindness of ordinary people.

School and Play: How Kids Helped the War Effort

During World War II, while adults were deeply involved in the war effort, children across the world found themselves playing unexpected yet crucial roles in supporting their countries. Though too young to fight or work in factories, these children contributed to the war in ways that were both significant and inspiring. They learned quickly that the war was not just a distant event reported in newspapers or overheard on the radio; it was a daily reality that required the efforts of everyone, including kids, to help their families and communities survive the difficult times.

In schools, the curriculum was adapted to align with the war effort. Education took on a new purpose, as teachers incorporated wartime themes into lessons, ensuring that children understood the importance of their contribution to the national cause. Math problems involved calculating rations, geography lessons focused on identifying battlefronts, and history classes were centered around the causes and implications of the conflict. These lessons were not just academic exercises but also a way to prepare children for the world they were growing up in—a world where every ounce of effort counted toward the collective goal of victory.

Beyond their studies, schoolchildren were encouraged to participate in various war-related activities. They took part in scrap drives, collecting everything from old newspapers and metal scraps to rubber and tin, all of which were vital materials needed for producing war supplies. These drives were often organized as competitions between schools or classes, with the winning group receiving a small prize or recognition. The sense of accomplishment and pride in contributing to the war effort motivated children to go door to door in their neighborhoods, often pulling wagons piled high with recyclable goods. These efforts, though seemingly small, accumulated into a significant contribution to the resources needed for the war.

Children also participated in Victory Gardens, an initiative that encouraged families to grow their own vegetables to reduce the pressure on public food supplies. Schools often had their own gardens, and students would spend time tending to the plants, learning about agriculture and the importance of self-sufficiency. These gardens were not just about producing food; they were a symbol of resilience and community spirit. By contributing to the garden's success, children felt a deep connection to the war effort, understanding that even their small hands could make a big difference in ensuring their country's success.

Playtime, too, took on a different meaning during the war. While games and sports remained a vital part of childhood, they often reflected the realities of the time. Children played games like "Air Raid," where they would practice ducking and covering as if a real air raid were happening, or "Soldiers and Spies," which mirrored the conflict they heard about from adults. These games were more than just play; they were a way for children to process the anxiety and uncertainty that came with living through a global conflict. Through play, they learned teamwork, strategy, and the importance of staying calm under pressure—skills that would serve them well in the unpredictable world of wartime.

Despite the challenges, children found ways to support the troops directly. Many schools organized letter-writing campaigns, where students wrote to soldiers on the front lines. These letters, often filled with drawings, stories, and words of encouragement, were a lifeline for soldiers who were far from home and longing for a connection to the world they were fighting to protect. The letters reminded the soldiers of what they were fighting for and provided them with a much-needed morale boost. For the children, knowing that their words could bring comfort to someone in a dangerous situation made them feel like they were truly part of the war effort.

Rationing was another area where children played a vital role. Food, clothing, and fuel were all in short supply, and families had to make do with less. Children were taught the importance of not wasting anything, whether it was food, clothing, or other resources. They learned to be creative, finding new ways to use old materials, and they helped their families manage the limited resources they had. Schools often held lessons on cooking with rations, teaching students how to prepare simple, nutritious meals with what little was available. These lessons extended beyond the classroom, as children took on more responsibilities at home, helping their parents with household chores and ensuring that nothing went to waste.

In some countries, children were also involved in raising money for the war effort. They participated in war bond drives, where they encouraged their families and neighbors to buy bonds that would fund the military. These drives were often accompanied by school events, such as performances or fairs, where children showcased their talents to raise funds. The sense of pride in contributing to something as important as the war effort was palpable, and these activities helped instill a sense of responsibility and patriotism in the young participants.

The war also brought children closer together, fostering a sense of camaraderie and shared purpose. In many cases, children who might not have interacted with each other before found themselves united in their efforts to help the war cause. Whether it was working together in a Victory Garden, collecting scrap materials, or writing letters to soldiers, these activities built strong bonds among the children, teaching them the value of teamwork and cooperation.

World War II was a time of great challenge and uncertainty, but it was also a time when children learned that they could make a difference, no matter how young they were. Through their efforts in school, at play, and in their communities, they contributed to the war effort in meaningful ways. These experiences not only helped their countries during a time of need but also shaped their character, instilling in them a sense of duty, resilience, and the importance of working together for a common cause. These stories of how kids helped during the war remain a testament to the power of even the smallest contributions when united under a shared purpose.

www.ingramcontent.com/pod-product-compliance
Lightning Source LLC
Chambersburg PA
CBHW060905140726

47996CB00001B/119

9 798330 391417